# *I Keep Thinking I'm You*

**Thomas George Santhinagar** is a prolific writer and poet. He has won several awards including the Hindi Prachar Sabha Award in 2014, and the Souhrida Samiti and Navarasam Sangeetha Sabha Awards in 2016. He is also a renowned translator, translating works from English to Malayalam. He has translated more than a dozen books of authors such as Albert Camus, Kazant Zakis, Tomasi di Lampedusa, Joseph Roth and Shashi Tharoor.

He is a retired chief engineer, who has worked for both the Government of India and the Government of Abu Dhabi for over thirty years. He has travelled extensively in Europe, the United States and China.

He is married with two children and three grandchildren.

# I Keep Thinking I'm You

Thomas George Santhinagar

RUPA

Published by
Rupa Publications India Pvt. Ltd 2019
7/16, Ansari Road, Daryaganj
New Delhi 110002

*Sales centres:*
Allahabad Bengaluru Chennai
Hyderabad Jaipur Kathmandu
Kolkata Mumbai

ISBN: 978-93-5333-420-8

First impression 2019

10 9 8 7 6 5 4 3 2 1

The moral right of the author has been asserted.

Printed at Parksons Graphics Pvt. Ltd., Mumbai.

*Some books are to be tasted,*
*Others to be swallowed,*
*And a few to be chewed and digested.*

—FRANCIS BACON

# Contents

# 1

## The Faculty of Eyesight

The man who had been born blind was sitting by the road, begging. His sharp ears were able to recognize a rustling sound emanating from the holy robe of the Miracle Healer. So, without restraint, he cried out, 'Jesus of Nazareth, please take pity on me, please…'

Jesus stopped and took pity on him. Knowing the answer, Jesus asked him, 'What do you want from me?'

He replied, 'Lord, please give me eyesight.'

Jesus spat on the ground and made some mud with the spittle. He rubbed the mud on the man's eyes and said, 'Go and wash your face in the Pool of Siloam.'

The man went there and washed his face. He then opened his eyes and was euphoric: he was able to see. With exhilaration, he jumped and shouted repeatedly, 'Jesus cured me of my blindness.'

This healing process took place on a Sabbath, which

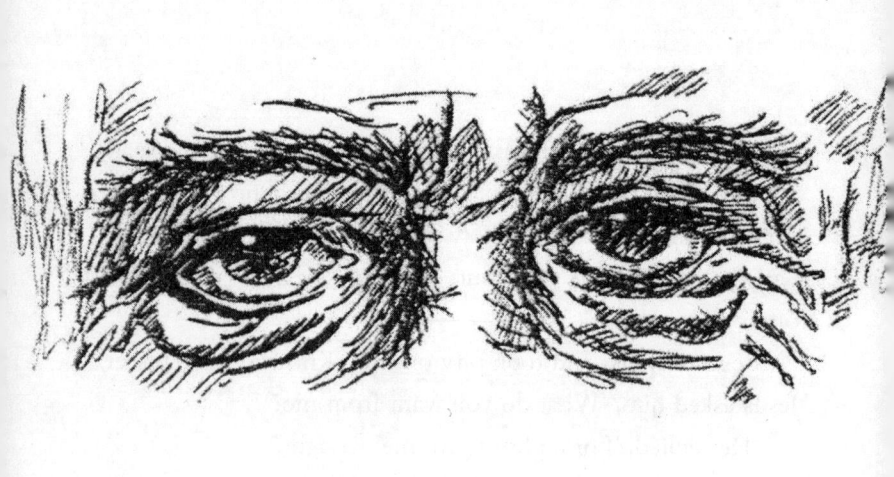

according to the Law of Moses, was meant only for worship and rest. Now Jesus was defying that Law. So the teachers, who were the authorized interpreters of the Law, flew into a rage. But Jesus asked them composedly, 'If anyone of you had a son or an ox that happened to fall into a well on a Sabbath, would you not pull him out at once?'

They had to keep mum.

After some time, the man who had got his eyesight back hurried back to Jesus. He was pressing his head with his hands and crying. 'Master, I have got a monstrous headache.'

'Because of your new eyes?'

'Yes, master.'

'Why?'

Then the man requested Jesus, 'Great Master, please save me. When the teachers tried to torture me for having got cured on a Sabbath, I was able to resist them boldly. But what I saw with my new eyes gave me the greatest shock of my life. I am downright desperate. Those leaders of society, who love to grab the reserved seats at feasts and temples, were squeezing very poor people to extract heavy taxes under duress. If someone could not pay, they were brutally beaten to death. Also, they labelled intractable, non-submissive young ladies as harlots and got them stoned to death. And I saw many more such atrocities. Lord, my innocent eyes cannot bear such evils. So please close my eyes forever.'

For a moment, Jesus contemplated and remembered two similar cases. One, an artist changed the positions of eyes in his sketches to present an exactly opposite expression. Two, a man, with two large holes in the place of his eyes because of a major accident lamented, 'I am unable to express my deep sorrow through my eyes.' And here was the third case.

Jesus took pity on the man again. He looked up to heaven and prayed, 'My Heavenly Father, those mischief-makers fully know what they are doing. Even then, Father, please forgive them.'

After this prayer, Jesus paused for a moment. Then he extended his hand heavenwards and brought down two long and sharp nails. Jesus then pierced those two nails simultaneously into the man's eyes. He was thus made blind as before.

Jesus wept.

After a pause, Jesus laid his hands on that man's head and said softly, 'My dear son, go ahead confidently, without stumbling anywhere, go ahead with an unruffled mind.'

# 2

# The Fire-prone Girl

When she was twelve, a fire caught her for the first time. The occasion was a clear morning. She was standing in her garden in front of a statue of a young man who was playing the flute. The sun's rays falling on the rose petals transformed them into a resplendent red. The fire enveloped her. The fire was a bright blaze of vermilion and appeared to have the softness of delicate silk. Terribly confounded, she cried aloud.

In the dead of night, bats used to fly into her garden. They ate and scattered pieces of guava, wax apple and other fruits. There was a coat of mist on grass blades and a mild cooling breeze. There were jasmine flowers as white as angels. She would sniff their scents. She would often lie down on the grass imagining herself to be a pearl shining in the sacredness of innocence. Such was her morning ritual and practice.

Now, before getting entrapped by the fire, she had seen a firecracker hovering incessantly over the head of the statue. She was tempted to jump and grab it. After many attempts, it was finally in her palm. Soon, all the other incidents followed: the fire wholly enveloped her; she cried out in terror; her mother came running hurried and worried, scooped her up and laid her on the bed. She wanted to tell Mom that she had seen a spark of fire on the statue's lips.

She did not witness the base of the statue getting burnt and the statue toppling into the mud.

Earlier, she had heard the statue speaking to her. She herself had, on many occasions, confided her complaints to the statue. In her pleasant mood, she had many a tête-à-tête with the statue. She used to sing and dance in front of it and thus entertain it. Also, she had hidden under its footstool, broken pieces of her bangles, peacock plumes and bits of her jottings. Neither rain nor shine nor wind had disrupted them.

She regained her vigour and cheerfulness four days after the fire. And on her visit to the garden, to her dismay, she understood that her perfect companion, the statue, had been subjected to a series of traumatic journeys. He had travelled from the garden to the roadside, to the waste bin and then into a limbo!

When she next attended her tailoring classes, her first task was to invoke the memory of her dear statue and make a large cotton-stuffed silk doll. She adorned him with an embroidered overcoat and expensive perfumes. She made a headgear for him with strands of her own hair. She then projected all her girlish dreams onto him. Then she whistled some romantic tunes and woke him up.

When she was fifteen, a fire caught her a second time. In the very early morning of a cold month, she felt like sitting near a campfire. The atmosphere filled her heart with enthusiasm. She looked up and started counting the stars spread out in the night sky. But then, somehow, the swing of a magical, mysterious dream lifted her up and threw her into the fire pit. At that time, she was holding very tightly onto her dear doll. What then? The fire relentlessly ate up her doll and one of her right fingers. The fire did not care a hoot about her loud cries. She felt heartbroken. She sobbed for a long time. Two blackened lips, two dimmed eyes and a highly choked dry throat were her balance sheet.

Then the third episode: She and her boyfriend walked arm in arm like lovers. She beamed a charming smile. After that they went on a jolly ride on his bike. She was the pillion rider. During the ride, when he started humming a melodious rhythmic tune, she sang along. They were lost in their own private world. She held her hands tightly around his stomach and pressed her developing breasts close against his back.

The motorbike rode down a steep slope after climbing a steep ascent. She was seventeen then. They were going too fast. The bike somersaulted and soon entered a tent of fire. Her boyfriend and the motorbike were caught in the flames. He went straight into the cave of death. However, she was thrown away from the bike into a sand dune. She regained consciousness only after a day. The accident had damaged her skin and the flesh of her heels and ankles, and they now resembled charcoal. Slowly she understood the gravity of the mess she was in. Her friend's loss severely upset her. She felt that her body was fully chained, and she had been dumped in a dark dungeon. The wounds on her legs were souvenirs of that calamity.

There was a tall tree, a weeping willow, in her backyard. It was symbolic of an impassioned state. In the evenings she would sit under it and ponder over her past and weep silently. With tearful eyes and a lot of incense, she paid commemorative homages to her old statue, the cotton doll and her deceased friend.

She was twenty when she was caught in fire for the fourth time. It was after she got married. She had received a nuptial string with a pendant. To her it was a symbol of something that would bind her and keep her in darkness. The bridegroom was an egotist who drew a very high salary. He came with all pomp and pride and made her his bride. 'One day, I will take you permanently out of this mouldy, stinking land to a sophisticated place,' he whispered into her ears when they were in the bridal chamber. She shut her eyes shyly with a smile. Her husband had slightly bluish beady eyes, porcupine-like hair and a pencil-thin moustache. He strode like an arrogant warhorse. He was the opposite of her. She wanted to change him. And to forget all of her negative thoughts, she would often hum a tune. Listening to that, he laughed as if he were in front of a clown in a circus tent. She was terribly hurt by this behaviour. She clenched her fists and gnashed her teeth.

Soon after her marriage, she started attending an embroidery class. She then slowly diverted her attention to stitching. In fact, she could stitch so well that she was soon making men's garments and accessories using embroidery and ornamental lace. When she presented him with an embroidered handkerchief bearing his name stitched with gold and silver threads, he started to behave more like a gentleman. And she was encouraged to experiment more with needlework. An extraordinary sweater, a pair of woollen gloves and socks, a monkey cap and a muffler were her immediate gifts for him. She derived great pleasure by giving him these items with her own designs. Although her husband's behaviour towards her gradually softened, he appreciated her handiwork to very few visitors. For them, he would display some embroidered pieces as if he was holding a public sale. He would say, 'This is the craft of my talented wife.' She did not want to hear such praise. Apart from these rare moments, she bracketed him together with the first citizen of the nation, since he seemed so busy. He used to come home very late in the evenings, which she hated. She wanted to erase this habit of his. She thought, '*Without bossing over me, he must take a break from his tedious routine!*'

He used to express his stress in murmurs. 'My planned schedules are getting worse day after day.' But she was helpless. She could only sympathize with him. 'What a nasty life!' she cursed herself.

One day, she received a letter from her old classmate. The letter had a photograph of her classmate's cherubic three-month-old son. She took that picture, went to an isolated part of her house and broke into tears.

That evening, she showed that picture to her husband with tearful eyes and a grieving heart. He realized the profundity of her grief. With a long face, he embraced her, but she moved away.

Later, she told him to change his hairstyle and the shape of his moustache. Further, she advised him to keep a smiling face always. She hinted that then everything would turn out to be lucky for them. Like a very obedient student, he conformed to her instructions.

Seeing him a changed person, she leaned on his chest and demanded of him, 'See, we too must have a child.' He seemed totally taken aback.

After an hour, when she went to the kitchen, he accompanied her. Noting his pleasant mood, she showed him an illustrated book about pregnancy. He was all smiles. She looked at his face closely and suddenly felt very bewildered. His face resembled the faces of her statue, her doll and her late boyfriend. Beads of perspiration started to break out on her forehead, face and armpits. A shiver ran down her back. In a moment, she swooned into him. A dense smoke of cloud was overpowering and suffocating her.

Their neighbours all rushed in. They found her beating her chest and weeping. In fact, she was rendered speechless. Scalding hot tears ran down her cheeks. She was totally unable to explain how the gas stove had exploded and killed her husband, and how her right palm had been severely burnt and carbonized. She was absolutely helpless to comprehend the cause of the whole calamity. In silence, she pleaded, 'Oh Fire, what I've lost is my heart. Please give it back.' She wondered which devil on earth was scolding her so cruelly with the flames of fire. She applied ointments on her burns and scalds. The cut on her forehead scarred over. She sat down with her head resting on her hands, muttering to herself, 'I don't understand anything; I don't understand anything at all.'

Her heart was heavy, her mind was exhausted and her back was bent. She sat alone in the darkness wearing widow's weeds, swallowing uncontrollable agony like the speechless statue, like the unsmiling doll.

# 3

# I Keep Thinking I'm You

What does Grandpa know? Grandpa knows simply to sit on the wall like a shadow! What does Grandpa know? Grandpa knows to leave me alone in this hell and make me cry at night. Hey, what did Grandpa do? Well, what did he not do? What did he not do that he ought to have done! Grandpa knows to make me lie alone and cry at night.

Grandpa will come near my bed and call me, 'David, my dear son!'

Then I'll happily respond, 'Yes, Grandpa, here I am!'

Grandpa would then lie close to me and caress me. Relishing that sweet comfort, I would slowly drift into sleep. I now grope in the dark for the long and slender arms of Grandpa, but I do not find them. Instead, my trembling hand descends on an empty nest of a bird. I hear the wailing of a feathered friend from a yonder tree. I sit on my bed and sigh in grief. Then I perceive devils with pointed horns and horrible canine teeth. Then on some distant beach, I see a walking stick, a pair of

sandals and a pair of long-sighted glasses! My dear Grandpa, where are you, where are you? Grandpa knows only to make me lie alone and cry at night... Grandpa is my grandpa and I am his only grandson.

Thus started and ended one night in the life of little David—a nightmarish dark time.

Grandpa was a solitary warrior in his youthful days. When he was eighteen, he left his poor family and native land and went to the High Ranges alone. There he conquered a vast stretch of barren land. He single-handedly fought against fierce animals like tigers, lions, leopards and wild boars. He also killed many poisonous snakes. Then there was an unexpected major landslide. He had to run for his dear life. He hid himself in a ravine for two days and nights! He had tamed some monkeys and dogs. They were his only assistants in the early days. His abode was on a tree and he stayed there for a few years. He had also made some watch huts on some treetops.

Later on, he built his own cottage, brought cows and sheep and then found a girl. But his married life was very short. Soon after giving birth to their son, Simon, his wife died. There had been no midwife to receive the newborn or to take care of the young mother. There were no other houses in the neighbourhood too. Grandpa was heartbroken. But then he mustered courage and determined to bring up his child alone. He did not trust that a new woman would treat his son as her own! So he did not marry again.

As that region slowly developed, people migrated to the land, Grandpa was anointed their leader. The new arrivals did not have to suffer even one-tenth of what Grandpa had undergone to convert the land into a fertile one. He also guided the inexperienced farmers.

When his son Simon was old enough to marry, he found himself a nice girl Alice and tied the knot. And in due course, to the new couple was born David. Me. I fully understood how Grandpa had developed the small kingdom we lived in. Grandpa was the uncrowned king there. He was the master of all that he surveyed.

When I was about seven years old, Grandpa started developing age-related ailments, like rheumatism and asthma. After a year, Grandpa was badly in need of treatment. There were ointments and physicians, but they needed money to provide treatment.

Grandpa and I do not have money on us. The one person with money was Grandpa's son and my papa. But that person was not touching his wallet. Why? Because he was a henpecked husband. His wife had drawn out a square on the floor and has asked her husband to stand within it! He humbly stands in it. Then she asked him to shake his head. Now he goes on shaking his head without stopping. He is adept at the art of shaking his head.

Grandpa used to tell me, 'Son, you've to swim like the smartest fish in the lake. And when you are running, imagine that you are a graceful bird that flaps its wings and flies by scooping out all the wind around it.'

Grandpa used to make big and beautiful kites and both of us used to fly them from the hilltop. Grandpa was also adept at driving out bandicoots that gnawed underground tubers. A shrill noise made while brandishing a stick with a long cord at its end frightened those creatures away.

Grandpa was very kind to domestic animals. He cared for them as if they were his own children. But finally what happened? Grandpa died a street dog's death! Grandpa's lingering look always haunts me!

Once, when the sky was crowded with thick black rain clouds, Grandpa said that they were clusters of heavenly rocks. When there was a nerve-shattering thunder, Grandpa said the angels were beating their drums. That was followed by a bright flash of lightning. Grandpa said that it was how God messages us. Grandpa knew to read all of God's messages! I had asked him then, 'Grandpa, please tell me, what's that message?'

'God is warning us. He says unless we stop hating one another, he'll send fire to burn us!' Grandpa had said.

On the third day after Grandpa's death, when I came back from school, I found that my mother's elder brother, who had recently retired from the Army, was occupying Grandpa's room. It seemed that he would be a permanent resident there. What deeply grieved me was that this man had thrown away Grandpa's walking stick, sandals and spectacles. I could not control my fury. I shouted, 'Which creature did this nasty act?'

My mom thrashed me severely, saying, 'Will you repeat this arrogance?' I did not reply even after many beatings. I called Grandpa for help and finally wept myself to sleep.

In the absence of Grandpa, in the profound void left by his passing, my sensitive mind ventured to look for his presence in my study, in the playground, near pond, on a hilltop, in my bedroom, at the dining table and anywhere else I could think of. However, this turned out to be a futile effort because ultimately, I was seeing cemeteries everywhere. The gurgle of the brook, the chirp and twitter of the birds, the gentle whistle of the breeze in the bamboo grove by the lake side all appeared to be mourning over Grandpa's departure.

I used to always imagine my Grandpa like a strong and tall tree, one that would never wither away! But now that he was gone, I felt as if I was a mere crevice in a dilapidated compound wall, ready to fall down at any moment!

One evening, I was returning home after extra classes in school. As I was approaching the gate, I saw my neighbours heading towards the living room. The sky was loaded with clouds and there was a flash of lightning. I knew that the message was being written, not by God, but by Grandpa. I read the message, 'Dear son, David! Wait for me! I'm coming down!'

All the neighbours were whispering something. My parents looked embarrassed. Why? The mystery revealed itself to me later. During his old age, Grandpa had been banned from entering the parlour because my mother did not want a dishevelled person disturbing its arrangement. And now look on the wall of the very parlour! Who is there? It is a full-sized royal figure of Grandpa as the patriarch with a long, overflowing beard and glittering eyes. He was the uncrowned king of the land and looks exactly how I always wanted him to appear. The neighbours murmured, 'Grandpa has come down to teach his son and daughter-in-law a proper lesson! What ungrateful treatment they had meted out to their father!'

With a heavy heart, my father rushed to the parsonage and brought the priest. A decent bedstead was arranged with a fresh bedspread and pillows. It was to be the tomb of Grandpa. The Bible was placed on the pillow. On either side of the cot, candlesticks with burning candles were installed. The priest prayed and sang hymns. And waving the censer, with its burning incense in it, he walked three times around the cot. He then blessed some pebbles and gave them to my father to bury in the four corners of our plot of land to get rid of evil. While taking his leave, the priest advised my parents to keep the candles burning for forty-one days, to pray for ten minutes in the mornings and evenings by standing at the foot of this tomb and to visit three holy churches and donate generously to them. The priest did not forget to accept the fee for his visit, prayer and the special exorcising action.

Without fail, my parents strictly followed this advice. Every morning and evening my parents stood by the tomb and prayed with all sincerity. 'Oh our Lord Almighty, the creator of both heaven and earth, truly, truly, we beseech you. Please incline the sky and come down to us, the sinners! Please wipe off our sins from us. Please deliver us from evil. Kindly forgive us all our mistakes and sins, which we had committed against our dear father, knowingly or unknowingly. As a sign of your forgiveness, please erase this big shadow from our wall. Amen.'

Right from day one, since the shadow had appeared on the wall, after coming back from school, I, with great exhilaration, would kneel down in front of it, imagining that Grandpa was lovingly caressing me.

Finally, the forty-first night arrived. It was a blue, moonlit night. My parents and I were in front of the shadow. Right before our eyes, with a slight hissing noise, the shadow was slowly vanishing from the wall. My parents wept with joy and lifted me up and kissed me on both cheeks. They always used to scold me for keeping Grandpa company and so this display of affection was out of character. I was now fully aware that Grandpa had returned as a happy and content soul after having received the respect he always deserved.

The next day's newspaper carried a full page obituary with a photo of Grandpa. 'In Fond Remembrance of Our Extremely Beloved Papa'.

I said to myself, 'What a great posthumous honour! Not at all bad, not at all bad! I felt like a frolicsome lamb. What amazing things a shadow can do!'

My face brightened up. Finally, I chanted, 'Grandpa, I keep thinking I'm you!'

# 4

# The Daily Bread

'Let the child come to me and I will not stop him. Because the Kingdom of Heaven belongs to such children,' said Rachel. She laid her hand on the head of the child and sighed.

Rachel relished the child's cool shadow and slept under it. The child blew a breeze and Rachel received its gentle caressing and felt a rapturous horripilation. The child and Rachel were in an island, which nobody else could enter. The fact is that no one else liked to enter there. That was why Rachel had announced boldly that the Kingdom of Heaven was with the child. 'Lord of Heaven and earth, I thank you for revealing that secret to this unlearned girl while you have hidden it from the wise and the learned. I know Father, this was how you wanted it to happen.'

For a child there are umpteen ways to cry. And for Rachel there is only one way to silence his cry: Just silence his cry, that's all.

Why is the child crying? Has he fallen down? Is he hungry? Does he feel pain? Does he yearn to see his parents? Is he starving for affection? Did he not get enough candy or was he not taken to the amusement park for a ride on the roller coaster? 'You saucy child, sleep now! Don't put your tongue out at me!'

Did Rachel shout like that? Did the dream of the child lead to horrible scenes, sobs and wailings? Fiddlesticks! Then why is Rachel employed here as his nurse? She has to look after this infant! Then what else the mother is doing? Is she employed? Not at all? Is she sick? No. Then? Phew, if the mother takes up that duty, then who will be there to conduct the fashion show, speak in the Women's Club about parenting, judge the mimicry competition, gossip about the behind-the-scenes-romance of the film world?

Is it true that the child's mother had a brilliant career? And as a housewife she was experiencing a void, so she resorted to social life to fill it? Now every month she appears in many discussions on television channels. Also she has to give many print media interviews. She cannot waste her precious time in changing napkins and feeding pap to an infant. These are duties, which any illiterate girl can perform! Are you Rip van Winkle to ask such silly questions without knowing anything about the modern world? Now, look at the child's daddy. The busiest man in town, with his finger in this pie and that pie. He's not just a mere busybody! He is sought by many up-and-coming men and women. He is the chief guest at major social gatherings. Isn't it clear that under such circumstances, the child and Rachel happen to be on an island? There, it's only about the child and Rachel! If somebody else enters, it's only with the permission of Rachel.

The sensible Lord has said, 'I assure you that unless you become like children, you will never enter the Kingdom of Heaven.' Rachel accepts this statement fully. To become like an infant, you have to consume infant's food in plenty! Why should Rachel sow and reap, and collect the harvest in the barn? If she is hungry, she has only to stretch out her hand, simply grab the food and eat! If the Lord says, what the right hand does, the left hand should not know, Rachel corrects it, 'What the hand and the mouth do, the eyes should not know.' So she closes her eyes like a cat and then eats and drinks. The hand can very well detect the route to the mouth! So she consumes a double scoop of ice cream in no time with eyes closed! If you ask her, 'What's the best way to stop milk going sour?' Rachel would reply, 'Simply drink it when it's fresh!' And she does it without her conscience telling her otherwise, although the milk belongs to the infant. Rachel has a huge appetite. A string in a garland of pearls can never become a pearl itself. By feeding the infant, Rachel will not get any nutrition. Her motto is: 'Eat nutritious food and digest it properly. Assimilate it into the blood to become ruddy.'

She had run away from a nunnery; she was a maid there. It was a mere drudgery and she became restless. From nunnery to nursery! The beginning was perfect and auspicious. Her taste buds became addicted to the infant food's flavour and ingredients. Enthusiastically she felt the rush of juvenile vigour and felt a thrill. Happily she drifted to the memory of her precious boyfriend, Benny, a smart and handsome student. He used to say she was his angel and goddess. He always used flowery words. 'My darling, you are my princess!' He injected in her youthful enthusiasm and intoxicating carnal desires. So the medium of baby food must be fully utilized. It is the shortcut to grace and charm! Easily digestible, with great calorific value. Unaffordable by ordinary folks. What a lucky abdomen! Benny used to passionately cajole her, 'On this planet earth, I've finally found that only your middle finger is fit for my wedding ring! So won't you wait for me?' But one day, with moist eyes, he bade her farewell citing an emergency and never returned. He left her with the sweetest memories. While thinking about him, her heart was not crying but was becoming a rock! Her womb was like a wasteland. But in all her dreams, there was a heart struck with a Cupid's arrow.

Now, Paul, the new driver of the house, filled the role of her romantic hero. 'My sweet dove, I love your buxom features. Don't ruin your looks. Know that nobody will request a dry cloud to give rain. Relax, fly like an angel by flapping your wings. Your luxuriant hair will flow in the air like a high tide.'

Rachel with her beautiful countenance was dressed in a gold threaded skirt and a thin matching blouse. Paul tightly encircled her hips with his arms. His smell pierced her nostrils. Intoxicated, she closed her eyelids involuntarily. He patted her on the head and then put a piece of cake into her mouth; she blushed crimson. They laughed and joked to no end. He would tell her lots of romantic tales with a twinkle in his eyes. She opened up and flowered into a frolicsome girl. Her flimsy silk blouse hinted at her high breasts with pointed nipples. He did not refrain from looking at her too closely and unashamedly. She too loved it. But soon Paul was transferred to the couple's estate. He left the island leaving his resplendent memories with her.

One afternoon, the devil in the form of slumber carried Rachel up to the top of a lush mountain. But then the child's shrill wails fell on her eardrums. The devil rolled her down the valley like a boulder. Rachel was upset. She was soon reminded of a folktale in which a priest thrust a nail into the skull of a blood-sucking fairy to overwhelm her. The wail of the child had disturbed her dream! She murmured, 'If I can tame this elf, I will be able to handle any devil! Don't try to play with me!' She squeezed the infant's tender skull and the wail tapered off. If the child does not drink its pap, it's not in Rachel's agenda to sing a nursery rhyme or tell a cartoon story and make the child drink it. For Rachel, the use of the silver spoon is either to crush a spider or to insert it into the throat of the child to stop it from weeping! Now to retrieve it, an operation is required?

On the whole, day by day, the child's condition is deteriorating whereas Rachel's health is improving in the inverse proportion. The child's mother neglected her duty; she never told her skinny son, 'You eat up my son, you look like a bag of bones!'

On a gloomy evening, on the child's birthday, there appeared bloodstains on the birthday cake. Also, the flames of the candles fixed on the cake got frozen whenever the child looked at them directly through his tears. Further, several holes developed in the birthday-balloons. Right then a physician was brought in. Before examining the child, he told Rachel, 'See Nurse, the child has a dirty pair of socks; his jacket is buttoned up on the wrong side! I have this strange feeling, if he swallows a bottle of ink, you'll use a blotting paper! If he bites his nails, you'll knock all his teeth out!' Then the physician lectured to the child's parents. He asked them why the child was not eating. Why only Rachel was eating? Both Rachel and the child were reported sick. And Rachel was eating more than double her required quantity. What's the psyche behind it? Instead of looking after her child, which was her moral duty, she became absolutely self-centred. Her illness emerged from within her. So its remedial measure must also come from within her. Her gluttony and make-up were all to convince herself that she existed! And now who will put her on a trial? The physician said that he would come after three days. Till then the parents must take care of the child and relieve Rachel from her duty temporarily.

Darkness gathers up everything! Rachel listened to the revelation of darkness. Then a nightingale whispered into her ears, 'Rachel, Rachel, in your short life you have seen a lot of love, a lot of laughter and a lot of tears. And now it is time for you to stretch out yourself on the floor as an invalid stamp paper. You were fully controlled by His Satanic Majesty.'

Then a priest came to exorcise her. He laid his hand on her head and prayed and chanted some hymns. Then he asked her to repeat a series of his own utterances. She simply obeyed.

The priest: 'I, Rachel.'

Rachel: 'I, Rachel.'

The priest: 'I hereby forsake Satan.'

Rachel: 'I hereby forsake Satan.'

The priest: 'I, Rachel...'

Rachel: 'I, Rachel...'

Rachel made a strange noise in her throat. She felt excruciating pain flooding out through her tears. Then her consciousness caught fire. A channel of blood and dribbling saliva found its way out from her mouth down her chin into the infant's daily meal....

Further, the aroma of all the child's juice she had poured down her gullet in the past seemed to hover around the infant. Rachel's black straight hair shook with her sobs.

# 5

# Robbery

Everywhere the sun blazed! But alas the whole atmosphere was of bewilderment! The tale of the loss of paradise was heard in every nook and corner. The first voice emerged from Moses, a poor farm hand. Only recently had he constructed a small house, through prolonged hard work. With a few more finishing touches, it would be a home. But before that could happen his house was subjected to robbery! It was a heart-rending sight to watch Moses growling like a dog at the thought of his heavy loss, the loss of his hard-earned money.

The crowd asked him, 'Moses, can you tell us what the robber looked like?'

Moses answered, shivering, 'He ran away through the dark! Off he went with the loot!'

But the crowd was relentless. 'In order to trace him, Moses, please tell us at least a bit about him.'

So Moses scratched his head and said, 'He was a giant, and I think slightly cock-eyed.'

Everybody felt slightly relieved. At least a fringe of evidence was at hand!

Lizzy was robbed next. She cried aloud non-stop, stating that she had lost the most valuable thing of her life. People rushed, nudged and surrounded her. They demanded, 'Lizzy, please tell how he looked like.'

Lizzy murmured, 'I don't remember anything at all. Don't you understand, I was just dozing off?'

The crowd was curious. 'Lizzy, at least tell us, was he as tall as you are?'

'Sure, he was slightly taller than me!' said Lizzy.

Someone piped up, 'What more can you add to that, Lizzy?'

Lizzy rolled her frog-eyes, scratched her nose and whispered, 'He had a brush-like moustache and a slight speech impediment'

'Anything else, Lizzy?'

'No, no, nothing more! Please leave me alone!' She resumed her wailing.

The next pitiable victim was the old widow, Mami. She had lost all her gold ornaments and other savings.

Mami said, 'I saw only a man who was lame in the left leg. He had turned the right corner and jumped away like a lamb. Do you mean to say that I should have ran and chased that fire-breathing monster in this advanced age of mine?'

'But Mami, was it possible that he was limping because of a sudden sprain in his leg?'

Mami said, 'Well children, I'm not an astrologer. What nonsense!'

'Right Mami, but, is there any chance that we can get his

handprints or footprints?'

'Oh yes, I say, there must be his tooth-prints.'

'Mami, what does that mean?'

'You twit, look at this. A mark of his teeth bite. Here is his half-bitten apple.'

The crowd found that evidence to be extremely useful. 'See, this is a main link in a chain of evidence. He doesn't have his left canine tooth.'

Mami scowled at the person who had asked the age of the robber.

Day after day, reports of thefts and crimes were heaping up, along with pieces of related, unrelated or fabricated evidence. An artist was brought in. He listened with rapt attention to all the eyewitness-accounts of the victims. Based on the data, the artist prepared a sketch of the criminal.

Looking at it a seminary student commented. 'It seems this crook boss was robbing Peter to pay Paul.' Many listeners did not understand what the student meant.

A boy, a voracious reader and a film fiend raised a pertinent question, 'Can't there be a gang with a criminal mastermind?' When no one answered it, he murmured to himself, 'A question is a question if it is answered judiciously'.

Ultimately, the Law and Order Department nabbed the 'criminal' based on the sketch, testimonies and circumstantial evidences because he matched every aspect of the accounts. It turned out that he was none other than the village chief.

At this realization the security chief said, 'What a piece of work is man! Okay, ladies and gentlemen, let's call it a day.'

# 6

## Mesmeric Advertisements

Each day is significant in its own way. If you are contradicting this statement, then you have all my sympathies! And I will conclude that you are simply enclosed in a cocoon. My dear pal, when will you wake up to think like me analytically and philosophically? Don't wait till your back becomes bent with age. If you observe closely, you will realize that each day of your life is unique in itself.

Look, there is a stranger coming towards me this morning. Should I avoid him? I can do that simply calling up someone on the telephone and then getting engrossed in a conversation about flatulence–price variations in different shopping malls, the latest sex scandals of political and cine leaders and other hot topics under the sun. If that option is not admissible, I can open an official file and pretend to be busy. Or else, I can straight away quit this official ambience and pace up and down the street looking at Humpty Dumpties, Little Nancies and Alices. Which one of these options should I choose? Well, none of

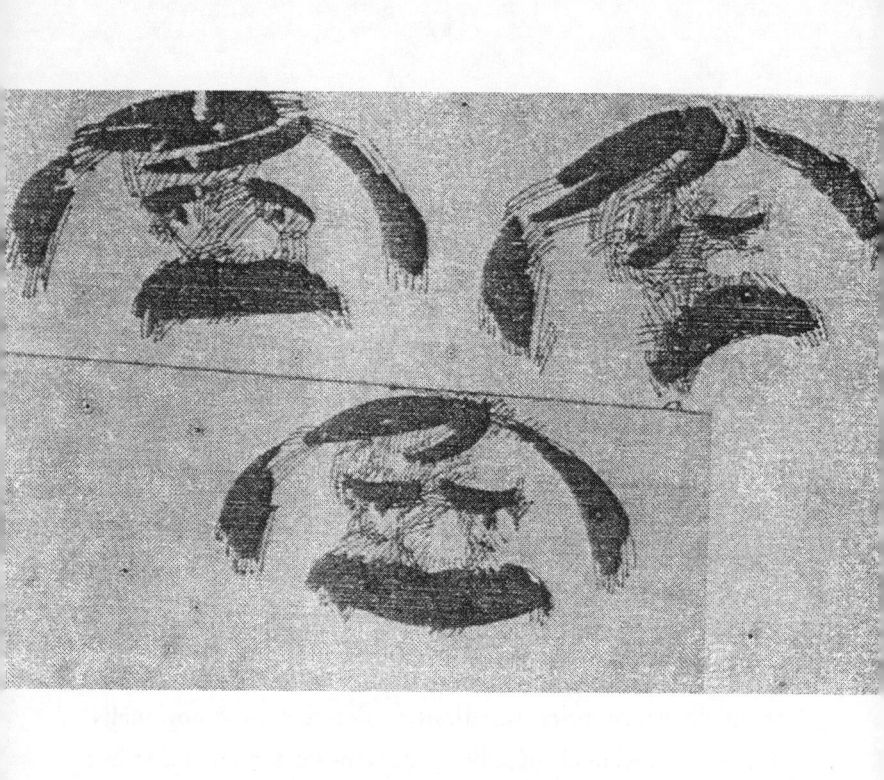

them. Because, today, so far, I have not served anybody. So, I turn my face to my strange and honoured guest with utmost affability.

Dear friend, come over to me. My heart is filled to the brim with dedication to serve you. See, goodness and mercy hold their hands and dance merrily in honour of your arrival. Oh, if I could attain the Kingdom of Heaven through such simple measures what a great bliss that would be!

Now, I look at your slowly approaching body with compassion. And the question I expect from you is this: 'Excuse me, is it possible to meet your chief manager now?'

But no, I am wrong, absolutely wrong. He hasn't asked for my manager but he wants ME, only ME!

I offer him a seat. He takes his place. Then he spreads before me a multicoloured glossy sheet of paper. He jabs his forefinger into the chest of a tabular form and announces, 'If you choose any one of these boxes, you will definitely land in the Alice's wonderland. If you are that infant Moses left in a reed box by the riverside in order to be saved from Pharaoh's sword, destiny will be that Pharaoh's princess herself will come to your rescue and bring you up in her harem as a prince!'

'Open your eyes wide and understand it, understand it fully,' he says.

Yes, dear, I understand it, I understand it fully: it is saving, ad, scheme and a window to the blue sky!

He emphasizes, 'Now just follow this.' He then flashes the torch onto various schemes and says forcefully, 'If you are dying after two years…'

'Stop! How dare you talk so rudely to me like that?'

He was stunned. 'Sir, I am from Life Insurance.'

'Please clear off! At the prime of my youth, I am unable to ponder over my after-life. If I must own my celestial abode in this fashion, my dear friend, I can outright discard it. Currently, I don't find time even to think about my present life, let alone about a distant, unknown existence. I am young, and a vast life lies before me! I must follow the line of least resistance and restore my mental balance!'

After his departure, I commanded my obdurate mind. 'From now on, do not look at any stranger affectionately.'

After a while, a handsome young man strode along the corridor. I admit that I am a fan of those who are aesthetically pleasing. So I fell for his charm and grace.

He asked, 'May I come in, Sir?' His voice was bewitching and his tone flattered my ego.

After taking his seat, he jumped into his narration. His company has come up with a fifty-volume encyclopedia set which will offer information about everything a modern progressive person must know at his fingertips. You can find everything you need using guidelines and you don't need the Internet to find a proper site. If you make a down payment, you can own the encyclopedia at 80 per cent. See, when you plant a tree, you plant coolness and shade. When you buy a matchbox, you buy a fire pit. When you buy a television, you transfer a fragment of the world's current affairs and entertainment into your living room. But if you buy this encyclopedia, what you really buy is the cosmos itself!

In all probability, I was bound to fall prey to such a tempting offer. But then I reminded him about the inertia of lazy teachers who simply throw up what they have studied or found in textbooks with no consideration to the individual aptitudes of the students under their charge. I also spoke about how when my son presented an enlightened essay on space travel, aliens and gene editing, he was jeered in the classroom. 'So my dear brother, for the children of middle class families that strive hard to meet the heavy expenses of rent, school fees, food, clothes, fare, medicines, this so-called up-to-date knowledge is an outright obscenity. If you sit here longer with your sermon you will aggravate my headache!'

I did not raise my head to see him off.

I reminded myself about my resolve. But then, behold, there was Joe, the son of my old classmate, Stephen. 'Come on in, Joe, come on.' I welcomed him heartily. Joe came in. He was all smiles. I suppressed my envy at his great success and prosperity about which his father had already told me.

And Joe relates to me with extreme meekness. 'Uncle, I've brought the most advantageous scheme for you.'

'Tell me Joe, tell me more about it.'

Joe went on. 'Uncle, if you take any article listed in this scheme, you'll get 12 per cent reduction in price. There's only one condition: You have to deposit a fixed annual amount to the company. So when others pay a hundred for an article, you need only pay eighty-eight. That's all.'

'Oh, great, really excellent. Truly VIP treatment from the son of my dear classmate. Yes, Joe, go ahead.'

Joe continued. He thrust a thick, golden card bearing somebody's handsome picture and signature in my hand. 'All the participants of this scheme will be provided with such special cards. You can use it to buy all your required articles at reduced prices from these listed outlets.'

He then unfolded a glossy booklet which categorized various commodities. The list included classy shopping malls, five-star hotels, super speciality hospitals, beauty parlours, restaurants, massage parlours, luxury car showrooms, pharmacies, furniture houses, opticals, sophisticated theatres, liquor outlets, gyms, sports and entertainment clubs and what not!

I scanned the list again. The places listed are the sort of places, which do not allow you to even peep at them from the outside without paying. Further, if from tomorrow onwards. I wanted to enter those fully air conditioned, and elaborately illuminated and decorated skyscrapers, and then make a deal, I would have to frantically discard my cotton clothes, herbal medicines and decoctions. I would have to switch over to top class textiles, special medical consultants, surgeons and antibiotics. Hereafter I would not associate with my usual wayside eateries. (Hey, Sir, your honourable seat in the revolving roof garden of the luxury restaurant is waiting for you. Please hurry up.) A tiger views a king or a beggar simply as a lump of flesh. These people are also tigers! 'My dear sonny, no, I don't need such extravaganza, simply because I have not matured to that superstar level.'

Last night, I found it extremely difficult to sleep because I was thinking about how in this virtuous world, the many liberal and generous souls standing in line only to help this poor creature out by offering large sums of money by way of installments, reduction sales, commissions and so on. Their sole aim is to make me rich!

What an interesting and amusing life it is when it is suspended from a cluster of sophisticated, mesmeric advertisements.

# 7

## Fever

'My laddie. My young son, why are you not sleeping?'
'Papa, I don't want to sleep. Papa, I am afraid I will have
those nightmares!'

For some a night is just to sleep and for others a night is
just to keep awake. In the middle of the night, Dany, a slip of a
boy, just six years old, lies sleepless on his bed. He is absolutely
uncomfortable, he is on the verge of wailing.

~

On a cloudy Sunday afternoon the trees in front of the house
appeared to be clowns shaking on stilts against the dark sky.
Andrew and Sarah were feeding their hens and sheep. Dany was
sleeping in the bedroom.

Then from the front lane and through their gate, there
entered a tall, well-built, muscular man of around thirty. He
was holding a striped canvas suitcase. On entering, he wished
them very politely, with a winning smile.

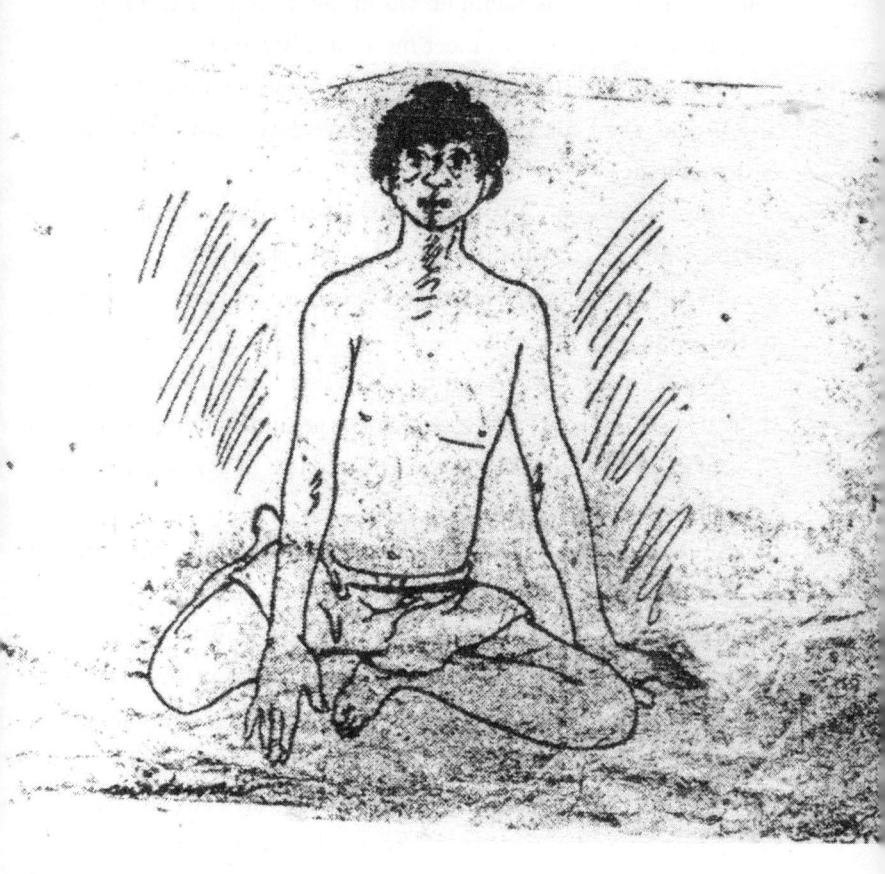

Andrew wondered if the man was one of his distant cousins.

But no. The newcomer says, 'I am representing Morrison Company, the wholesale dealers of domestic products as well as selected items for the feminine world. Sometimes, I carry out door-to-door sales also to meet my monthly target.'

Andrew broke in, 'Sorry! At the moment, we do not have any urgent need for your products. We always buy only our essential items.'

The visitor said, 'That's all right. I'm not the sort of sales person who either disturbs or compels my clients.'

'I've heard a clever salesperson knows how to sell ice even to the Eskimos.'

'No, no, never Sir. No modern salesman does that sort of thing. He gives priority to the customer's genuine requirements.'

Sarah interjected, 'Excuse me, I would like to have a general idea about your products.'

The visitor replied, 'The pleasure is mine, Madam. You can go through this brochure. I have only one copy now. And please feel free to ask me questions if there are any doubts. You can just note your favoured items and place the order any time later.'

Sarah took a full fifteen minutes to study the brochure with utmost concentration. Some of the items really did interest her. Meanwhile, Andrew was getting irritated. So he said, 'Mister, see, finances are tight so we cannot make any purchase now. Moreover, we have to wake up our son. He has to do his homework, which takes a lot of time.'

'Okay, I'll leave now. Anyhow, I just wanted to introduce our company's products to you. In this respect, I feel I was successful. So far, no door ever has been closed permanently on me. Now I must thank you very much for spending a few minutes with me. Have a nice weekend. Bye.'

~

A sleep that encourages laughing heartily, along with a sweet dream.

A sleep that has to be evaded because of the invading nightmares.

Dany sat on his bed with a face contorted with haunting febrile fright.

~

One evening, a week after the visit of the salesperson Andrew noticed that Sarah was in a very jovial mood. Suddenly he saw on her left middle finger, a glittering gold ring studded with an emerald gem. 'What's that new addition on your finger?' he asked.

Sarah said, 'Oh, I was about to tell you what had happened today. That salesman came today and gave me this ring. He said that it would be on a two-week's trial. If nothing unfortunate happens to the wearer, then only must we pay. Otherwise he would take it back.'

'But how much is the price?'

'Well, when I asked him, he said, that could only be stated if we accepted it. Also, he said that we could afford it.'

'But I don't grasp his psychology! And why should you wear an ornament without paying its price?'

'Oh, take it easy. It's only a trial. It's not a big issue at all. Moreover, if we do not want it, we can very well return it, saying that we found it quite unlucky. It is as simple as that!'

~

Ten days passed by as quickly as a flash of lightning. One evening, when Andrew came back from the office, he was shocked to see a gold chain with a heart shaped pendant embracing Sarah's long neck and her full, high breasts when she bowed down. He kept his cool for some time. Later, he asked, 'Sarah, is your new chain also on a trial basis? Is it for sale, if nothing unfortunate happens to you for a certain period?'

'That's right. I promised him to pay the price by selling a lamb. Then he told me not to hurry as he had to go away urgently on a mission. Saying so, he soon hurried off.'

Andrew kept mum. But he did not find the meal served before him tasty at all.

~

'Papa, Maggie was my close friend in my class. She used to tell me so many bedtime stories. We never quarrelled. I don't know why she went alone in the evening to that cemetery area to pick jasmine flowers. Uncle Jose said it was a cobra. Just one bite. Soon her body turned blue! Papa, I cannot sleep! I don't want to sleep. I see only Maggie's blue, still body and a big snake throughout my sleep. Papa, please, please, I don't want to sleep...'

'My dear little son. Don't think about those things. That is the only way out! Dany, now I'll make the sign of the cross on your head, and I'll pray for the merciful presence of the Lord at your head, Mother Mary at your feet and the six apostles each on either side of your bed. So the devilish bad dreams will never attack you!'

'But Papa, where's Mom? Has any demon taken her away? When will she return? If Mom were here, she could clasp me tightly. Then bad dreams won't touch me at all. I don't know anything Papa, I don't know anything. Maggie and snakes will not go away at all!'

'C'mon my son! You have heard my prayer. Believe it. And now I'll hug you tightly. Let's sleep together! Let's see who sleeps first! C'mon, get, set, go!'

~

When my lover beckoned me through the keyhole, I was so thrilled that I readily got up, grasped the handle and opened the door for him. Then from my long and slender fingers sweet smelling perfumed oil dripped onto the latch. His wine like mouth was sweet to kiss and everything about him enchanted me. My lover is mine and I am his. He had told me, 'My love, my dazzling dove, your eyes hold me captive.' Then in the dark hours of the night, he put me in a big basket, hid me and carried me on his head to the coolness of the lovely country fields. There we danced arm in arm to our hearts' content. Then the fever of our private passion burst into flame and burnt like a raging fire.

~

What a rude awakening! A young wife elopes with her secret lover forsaking her young son and husband!

~

The mother leads her son up the mountain carrying a bundle of firewood, live coals and a sharp knife. There, she ties him and places him over the altar of firewood. The boy pathetically asks, 'Mom, where's the lamb for the sacrifice?'

'What lamb? You're the lamb. You're the sacrifice!'

Then she raises the knife. A single cut. In a moment, the head and the body are in two parts![1]

~

Herod says, 'The three wise men have tricked me! They had seen the new star as the symbol of the birth of the king of Jews. But they didn't come back to give me a clear identification of the infant, my future rival. So I gave the order to kill all the boys aged up to two years!'

A sound is heard in Ramah, the sound of bitter weeping. All the Rachels are crying for their children. They refuse to be comforted, for their children are dead already. Their big breasts full with milk are smarting and yearning to suckle.[2]

'That's the case in Ramah. But here the case is entirely different! O, Dany, my son, you are not dead. You are very much alive and kicking! Now tell me this, are the breasts that suckled you and the womb that carried you really lucky?'

~

---

[1] A twisted reference to Biblical story: Abraham's attempt to sacrifice his son, Isaac (Old Testament).

[2] Related to Jesu's birth (New Testament).

Andrew kissed his son and then sobbed silently. 'Lord, I am prepared to hang on the cross upside down like Saint Peter for the salvation of my family. But Sarah, you are doomed! You need not weep for me! You weep only for yourself and your son!'[3]

Andrew's soul was feverish. Andrew's skull was burning in a red hot pyre. Andrew now falls into an infernal chasm and his face is contorted with haunting febrile fright...

---

[3]On the way to Calvary bearing his cross, Jesus advised the wailing women on the road side: 'Don't weep for me, but weep for yourselves and your children.'

# 8

## Life

We always enthusiastically looked forward to the arrival of our 'Grand Uncle'. He was around sixty-five. At that time I was a fourteen-year-old boy. My sister and brother were aged ten and seven respectively.

Uncle used to come to our house in the village once in a blue moon and stay for three days. His luggage would consist of two pairs of his clothes, a bath towel, a cake of soap, tooth brush and tooth powder.

Though our mother did not hate him, she did not welcome him either. For one, after his arrival, her children would not care to touch their textbooks. Two, she had a traditional mindset and wanted to respect her guest. She wanted to serve him only special dishes, and we had no domestic help. Mom did all the household chores alone.

On the contrary, Papa liked him very much. Mom had told us confidentially, 'Children, remember, he is not at all our blood relation. He hails from Papa's village, that's all!'

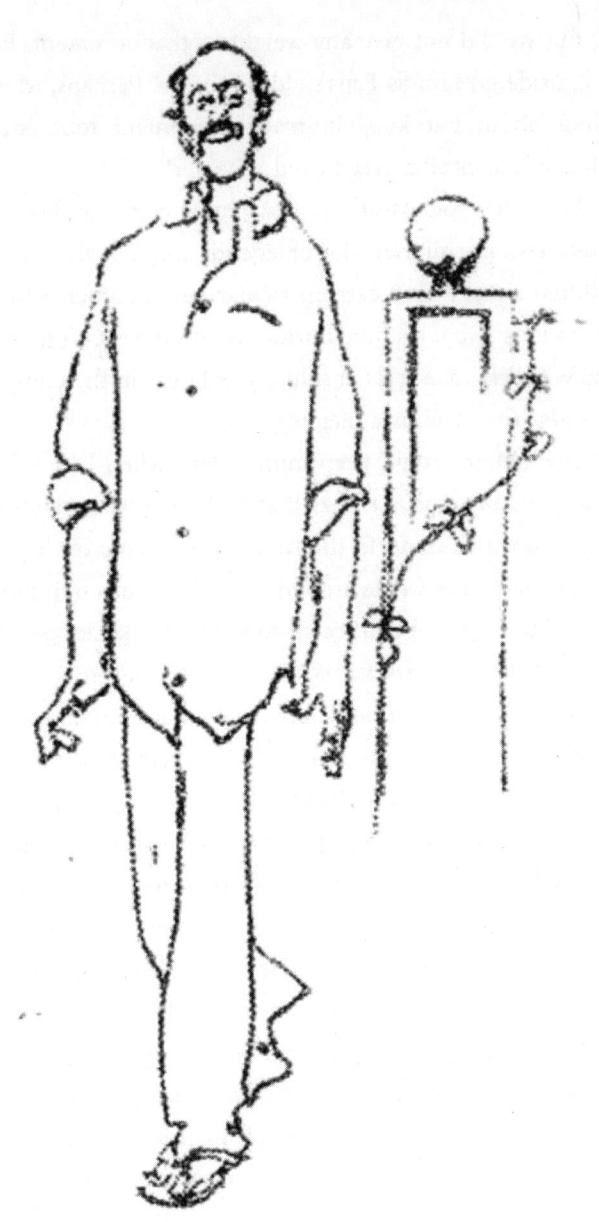

But we did not give any weight to that comment. Instead, we considered him as Papa's elder brother. Perhaps, Mom was jealous about her kids' intimate attachment to a 'stranger'. Jealousy is after all a green-eyed monster!

Papa once told Mom, 'Suja, when he comes and stays here, he teaches our children a lot of legends and folktales and songs. Children should have extracurricular entertainments too. And see, he mostly comes here during their holidays. Certainly that simple, lonely man feels absolutely at home in the company of our kids. That itself is a blessing to us.'

Then Mom would keep mum. Now, when I look back to those 'good old days', I realize that such understanding between couples was the secret to the tranquility of country life.

The next time Uncle arrived he looked worn out. But, then I thought, it would be indecent to ask such a senior person the reason of his tiredness.

One evening, after our supper, we sat around him. We were bubbling over with enthusiasm and anticipation. He told us thought-provoking stories, riddles, adventures of blood-sucking elves and about the escapades of notorious dacoits who were overwhelmed by village chieftains. Then he told us about his own experiences in distant places and his associations with different categories of people. He was indeed opening before our imagination scrolls of a magical wonderland.

The finale of his presentation ran something like this: 'My boss was a leading, established businessman and moneylender. Once he asked me to reach his stately mansion the next morning at five o'clock so that we could proceed together to meet his business partner. Accordingly, I reached there ten minutes before the stipulated time. I went upstairs to meet him. There, what a terrible scene I witnessed! The robust body of my boss was lying there, lifeless, with bulging eyes and in a slimy pool of blood! A long, sharp knife had pierced deep into his abdomen.'

'Eh?' We all asked together with a shudder.

'Who stabbed him?' asked Joel.

'How to know that? My boss was a famous billionaire. He had a lot of envious rivals. Or it was the work of some roguish robbers.'

Lily asked, 'Then what did you do?'

'That day I left that place once and for all.'

The detective in me woke up and said, 'The security guard would soon inform the police who could come in no time and nab the person found at the crime-site; or, perhaps the guard himself did this and then ran away. Uncle, how could you escape easily?'

'Well, Wilson, my boy! I couldn't sniff like a police dog. My only aim was to flee from the scene of murder. So I stealthily descended along the drainpipe, reached the ground, mustered up all my strength and courage and ran along a narrow, dark lane beside the garden. But my birth star betrayed me. The gardener shouted and two more people came running, they grabbed me, and then beat me black and blue without any sympathy. They were showing their loyalty to their boss by beating an innocent man!'

We asked in unison, 'Then what happened?'

'Then what! I died on the spot!'

I said, 'But you are not a ghost now! You've your life now.'

Then after a pause, with a choking voice Uncle asked us, 'My dear children, can you all call this life of mine a LIFE?'

Two drops of tears fell from his eyes.

The next morning when we woke up, we found that he was gone! We found out the next month that he had died naturally. Also, Papa informed us that although innocent, Uncle was imprisoned for many years and upon his release had been admitted in a mental institution where he stayed for about two years.

I asked Uncle's last question to myself: Was Uncle's life a livable LIFE? Oh, DEATH is the final leveller!

# 9

# I Travel Heavenwards
# in the Chariot of Time

It pained me a lot. I am really perturbed and sad. I can't stand such things for long.

First of all, you just make a note of my name. I am Tomy, a company assistant. I will tell you all. Then you'll come to know what a naive person I am.

My boss scolded me once again today. Scolded me severely. 'Irresponsible creature! Late again!'

His bootlicking manager supported him. 'Sir, is it something new?'

'You Tomy, you'll get the sack soon for being late!'

What shall I do? My fortune line has been rudely contorted right from my birth; my birth star has also sunk deep into a marshy land. Can Boss lift it up with a grapnel?

Every night when I get to bed, I earnestly pray to all the holy saints to make my next day an auspicious one. And in

the morning, I get out of the bed by making sure to plant my right foot on the floor first. I don't forget to cross myself before starting any work, great or small. But what to say? By the time I set foot in my office, that merciless solar disc, up above the world so high would have reached above my head! What for? Just to make me eat fire! Just to make my boss behead me!

See, I won't blame my boss who strives so hard to run the show and pay his staff promptly. He has to be a strict disciplinarian, a hard taskmaster, a dictator. One has to shed sweat and tears as well and know the trick of the trade fully well to make money. Boss keeps dogs to bark; he himself need not bark. But then what? Does he have any mental peace? Does he sleep well? Poor Boss! And if he gets angry with me, why should I get angry with him?

Now, let me tell you frankly. It seems I am destined to be a victim of rebukes. Here, a flashback seems very appropriate, Mom used to say, 'Oh, Lord, is there such a firstborn blockhead anywhere else on this earth?' Papa would endearingly say, 'You clumsy clown, go away, you are a pain in my neck!' My class teacher would say, 'Little Tomy is our Humpty Dumpty. He always falls off the wall. Tomy cackles often, but never lays eggs! When Tomy grows up, he will easily be an MD, a mentally deficient!'

One day I asked Master, 'Sir, why do you tell everybody that I'm a dullard?'

Master replied, 'Sorry Tomy, I didn't know it was supposed to be a secret!'

I never minded if the whole class made me a laughing stock. But I would quickly become gloomy if my Jill joined the others in laughing at my expense. But see, in what a high position Jill is now! And where is this poor little Tomy?

Let's come back to the reproof. In the past, when someone scolded me, I could not take that seriously at all! So I would stand still with my mouth wide open! Once in a while I might scratch my head. That's all. This surely angered them. I would resign to myself to whatever the future had in store for me. I never did this deliberately. It is my nature, just like leaves and parrots are naturally green.

But please take it from me. At the bottom of my heart, I yearn to be a prompt worker, accomplish all my assignments in time and report to office in neatly pressed dress. I want to win that Smartest Employee Award. Any of my well-wishers can engrave my above ambition on my grave stone!

~

Buy a watch, own a watch: that was my long-standing desire. But because I am a sensitive, generous, gregarious person, I was unable to say 'NO' to the demands of my old classmates and other country folks and would always gift them what they wanted. They would never understand me. They think I am a well-placed officer in the city. None of them has ever come to me saying they will guard my interests. So I lead an austere life and am contented knowing that they are happy upon receiving my gifts.

I did not want to harbour sour grapes. So I heartily went through the coloured catalogues of classic brands of watches. Then I realized that a watch adorning a male wrist was like ladylove lying on the broad chest of her man and constantly tickling him! The long and the short of it: I couldn't sport a watch yet. This poor Tomy of yours is like a line, with only length and without thickness! No weight at all!

~

Mine is a strange world. My rented cottage stands away on the road under a spreading tree. Fragrant flowers spring around my ivy porch. I am a lonely resident here. The only neighbouring house is under lock and key. My world is filled with an aching void. I felt like naming my cottage 'NIGHTMARE'.

One night I dreamt that I was hurriedly climbing up a mountain. And in a split second, I slipped and fell into a deep chasm. My head hit very hard on a gigantic gong. The ear-shattering sound woke me up. Suddenly I realized that the sound was real and was not coming from my house. I ran to the kitchen, stood on a stool and peeped through the ventilator. A new resident! The sound was her sneezing! Her handkerchief was dripping and she was still in the middle of a bout of sneezing. Without wasting time, I hurriedly finished my morning duties and rituals, and ran off to my office. My boss was wonderstruck! With satisfaction he beamed at me. I whole-heartedly thanked my neighbour, a buxom, middle-aged lady. Oh, she has become a rose without thorns! Her loud sneezing culminates in my reporting to the office promptly. I revere her and I'm even ready to worship the ground she walks on!

But one hitch: I was still bound to sit in the office until

eight in the evening. And I would not receive compensation for my early arrival. It will seriously affect my health if I have to sit longer hours every day!

~

Next Sunday was my washday. As I was taking a nap in the afternoon, I heard a knock on the door. I saw a female figure enter into the monotony of my bachelor life. In my dreams she was an ethereal, angelic form: her thick, dark hair flowed down to the floor and her rose coloured silk dress hugged her graceful curves. When she opened the door and entered my room, my dream was shattered! She was my new neighbour, that obese number. Immediately she asked, 'Do you know me?'

I said, 'Yes, I've seen you; my new neighbour.'

'Okay, now one urgent thing. Did you see my husband's moustache?'

I said, 'Yesterday I saw him, a very slim person, but I did not notice his moustache.'

Then she moved close to me. I feared that her high-heeled shoes would cause her to slip and that she would crush me. I offered her a strong chair. She sat and heaved a sigh and we introduced ourselves.

She continued. 'Yes, Tomy. My husband and I are mismatching, physically. After our wedding, he started getting thinner and I fatter. After our marriage, I came to know that he cannot sprout a moustache! How to present such a pencil-thin person without a moustache as my husband? I wept bitterly.

Finally, I got 'Stalin's moustache' made in a Singaporean wig factory. Seeing him fitted with that gives me great relief. Now, about my present visit. He removed his moustache and kept it on the bathroom's windowsill before taking a bath. A fat cat took it and ran off. We could not find it in our house. God will bless you, Tomy if you find it for me. Otherwise, I'll be heartbroken. Tomy, I've to tell you one negative aspect of it. From the day I arrived in our new house, exactly at six in the morning, I have been sneezing five or six times with an explosive sound. Tomy, is it a disturbance to you?'

How can I reveal the truth? My whole existence now hinges on that nerve-shattering sound! But I said instead, 'As a neighbour, it's all very tolerable.'

She said, 'God will bless you Tomy.'

Then hurriedly, I went on all fours to look for the cat in every nook and corner. I noted that she could not bend down. At last I found the strong, fat cat fully stretched on the kitchen ledge. It had fitted the moustache on its face! I took my fishing net and stealthily caught it and removed the moustache! The saddest part of this episode was that as soon as she saw it, she snatched it from my hand and flew back to her house without even wishing me goodbye! Later I blamed myself for expecting a tête-à-tête from her, simply for retrieving her missing stuff!

The next morning while going to office, I had taken a film magazine from my house to read during my lunch break. When I entered the office, my boss urgently called me to get an important document from his table. After a thorough search, I found it and gave it to him.

This surprisingly, marked an important turning point. I will come to that. At six o'clock in the evening my boss started sneezing five or six times with a heavy noise. I thought the lady-next-door had come to my office. My fat and aged boss was unable to withstand this physical strain. He was sweating heavily and was rolling his eyes with suffocation. His driver came running, lifted him and took him home safely. When my boss had left, I thought of snatching an expensive cigarette from his table. Then to my horror, or to my relief, there, I found my film magazine. In the morning when he had called me, it happened to slip from my hand. The funniest part is that my neighbour's moist handkerchief was within that magazine! I put on gloves, dropped the handkerchief and threw the magazine into the incinerator. From that day on my boss has sneezed like a bomb explosion at six in the evening every day and has had to go home. I coolly follow suit. Every dog has his day. I now get enough time for reading and yoga practice.

Now, in this age of robotics, every Tom, Dick and Harry has a wristwatch. So to set oneself apart, it's better to be without one. Moreover, by loving the watch excessively, I had started to hate it! I can now tell when it is 6 a.m. and when it is 6 p.m because of the two ticking time bombs in the form of my boss and the fat lady. My prayer: no physician should come forward to cure the lady and my boss of sneezing!

Do a great service by loving your neighbours free of charge as exemplified by the lady-next-door! You can think of some other options too!

See, I now travel heavenwards in the chariot of time!

# 10

## Going, Going, Gone!

The fight between the neighbouring countries had been going on for some years, before the advent of the digital revolution. The territorial army was fully deployed by each of the warring rivals.

The whole nation was on alert against any sort of attack from the enemy. Throughout the country there were processions and propaganda to whip up patriotism. It was important to tarnish the image of the enemy. Maintaining strict discipline was of supreme importance. Citizens were urged not to or listen or spread rumours. Codes of conduct to be observed by citizens during wartime were widely circulated. 'Donate generously to the war fund' was another major slogan. Voluntary agencies were collecting medicines, blankets, clothes and food items for the people of the war-torn areas. In every street corner there were spirited nationalistic speeches, songs, slogan shouting, etc. Every railway station in the country witnessed mammoth farewell functions as valourous soldiers left for the war front.

Fourteen-year-old Philip's father John was serving in the Army. Every soldier's family was in a state of tension throughout the period of war.

One day a message from the Army headquarters reached Philip's house stating that John had a heroic death. His widowed young wife fainted. After some days, she came back to her senses, but remained shell shocked for many days. Philip's kid sister stopped going to school and stayed at home to give her mother company. His mother's behaviour, her wild and vacant stares frightened him.

Philip started cursing the war. He cursed the destiny that forced his father to join the Army. He cursed the enemy country that killed his poor, loving father. He cursed his own fate that did not permit him to lead a normal boy's happy life.

After some months, a close friend of his father came home on short leave from the frontier. He covertly told Philip the startling story behind the death of his father.

During the war the Army headquarters had allotted fixed quantities of various items as ration to different units. An unpatriotic gang of officers in charge of the stores conspired with the suppliers for illegal adjustments like non-supply of the full quantities, supply of second grade items, adjusting non-supply with the existing stocks.

Philip's father detected these nefarious activities. Being a patriot, he was determined to report the matter to the authorities concerned. The traitors came to know what he was going to do.

There was only one way out for those culprits to save their own skin. They shot John from a shelter in the war front and made it appear like an enemy assault

Later, Philip sat in a wistful mood scanning through wartime newspapers spread on the floor. They issued bold warnings: 'This is wartime. Don't listen to rumours.' 'Minimize your spending. Practice austerity.' 'Donate to the war fund generously. Join hands to drive away our enemy!'

Philip wondered what the enemy meant to him. He took out his diary and wrote, 'They say war is barbarity, a savage cruelty, a heinous flood of blood and the only competition under the sun in which neither side wins. Also, in the war both sides delight in destruction. Apart from them, there are the pacifists who shout: 'Down with all wars! Down with all weapons of war!' Finally, I define the ENEMY No. 1 as the house that is divided itself into groups in order to fight or suppress.'

# 11

# The Confessor

Tuesday. A humid April night.

The vicarage is calm and quiet. After his long prayers and readings from the Old and the New Testaments, the aged vicar has just gone to sleep. A dim light shines in a remote corner of his bedroom. His cook has already gone home after serving supper. In case of an emergency, Father can seek the help of his neighbour Jacob, a member of his own parish. So far Father has no age-related health problems. He is of a cool temperament, and is very humane too. Also, he is a voracious reader and a good orator. In his speeches, he always uses ordinary words, examples and anecdotes from day to day life. This trait makes him very popular with the laity.

At three in the morning there is a gentle knock on his door. Quite unusual.

Father asks, 'May I know who wants me at this late hour, please?'

The visitor says, 'Father, I'm really sorry to disturb your

sleep at this untimely hour. But mine is a very urgent case. I've to make a confession and then go to a faraway place. I'll need only ten minutes, Father.'

Father had nothing to lose. He was successfully completing the race of life and thought that he was a deserving candidate for the eternal crown in his afterlife. If he did not accept this visitor, Jesus would be losing a son forever. So Father speaks aloud, 'Just wait please. I'm coming.' Then he slowly moves to the door and opens it. There is a middle-aged, bald man. Before studying the man's full form, Father says, 'You are welcome, come in please and take your seat.'

'Thank you, Father. I've heard much about you. You're to me that Jeanval Jean with the silver candlesticks?'

Father breaks into a hearty laugh and says, 'Be seated.'

The visitor said, 'No. Father, I'm not eligible to sit in yours presence. As we read in the Bible, I must say, I'm not good enough even to untie your sandals.'

Then Father laughs and says, 'My son, forget it. You are no John the Baptist and I am no Jesus Christ. Now let's get straight to the point.'

'Father, first of all, let me tell you that I'm not in a state of intoxication. I particularly chose you because you are co-ordinating many projects for orphans, widows and lonely, aged people. And I didn't want any intermediary between us. We want privacy in this matter. Father, please give me a patient hearing. Today, at midnight, I robbed a fabulously rich man's mansion. His family was away, and his security guard had gone to leave his wife at a hospital's emergency ward. Being alone, before going to bed, he had consumed a full bottle of whisky. The empty bottle was near his bed. After manipulating his internal security systems—see, it was due to my long-term planning—I used a set of duplicate keys, opened the safe and collected all the valuables and banknotes. It was all done stealthily and successfully. But, suddenly, as if by intuition or reflex action, he woke up and was terribly shocked to see a stranger in his bedroom.'

The visitor continued, 'As I had expected, he soon took out of his revolver from under his pillow. I'm a martial arts expert, so I ducked and overpowered him. I had to finish him on the spot. Then I dumped his body in the incinerator. Father, you must know about this crook. He had come up in life from scratch through unfair means—working as a pimp and in collusion with the underworld. His nexus with unscrupulous bureaucrats and politicians is notorious. He had made more than a dozen men, including my uncle, homeless. He had mercilessly spoiled many women, including my aunt. He was the uncrowned king of that locality. My blood always boiled whenever I thought about him.

The visitor was speaking like an orator, choosing words carefully with proper gestures. There was no interruption in his presentation. His listener never thought of diverting his attention away from the speaker's face, but the visitor stood holding his head high and without even shifting his legs. His expression was that of an energetic activist whose muscles screamed for activity. His posture was that of a veteran criminal lawyer in a court of law defending a murderer against all circumstantial evidence. He was not at all scared stiff.

The visitor continued, 'Father, without a weapon, a robber would be naked. And I believe that the best moral sanction is that of the conscience. Father, please take it from me, socialism will never be a reality. Communist China is a capitalist country. Now, regarding the purpose of my visit here, you need a lot of money for running your various projects. You cannot grab money as I do. Please accept a share of the money I've got—this donation is for my peace of mind. Father, actually this is capital levy. And Father, being a veteran in this field, I've left no clues for the police, even about my arrival here. Father, bear in mind that this is a confession and you are bound to keep its secrecy. Father, I'll admit this also: at the very moment of finishing off that crook, I experienced an orgasm of ecstasy.'

'One more thing, Father. All your bishops demand and accept hefty contributions from big sharks, knowing fully well that those contributions are unaccounted and illegal money. They don't ask donors about the source of income. I am not after publicity, and I do not claim to be a philanthropist. I am not a taxpayer, either. So you can utilize and spend this money in small amounts at a time. This money is exactly as if someone had left it at your doorstep. It's like how the money you get in your offertory. I know, the hand that gives, gathers. Father, I'm now taking leave of you. Thank you, Father, goodnight.'

He leaves. Father kneels down and prays, 'O, Good Lord, guide me with your divine light. Master, as you know, I'm a mendicant eligible for accepting alms from willing hands. I do not know what the boundary is in this case. But my conscience is pricking me. Two equally robust forces pull my mind in opposite directions. To be in the confessor's role or in the true citizen's role? Lord, please show me the light.'

# 12

## No More Teaching Session

There was a blackboard in the classroom with nothing written on it. But on the ledge of the board, there were pieces of chalk and a duster.

Derek, the class leader, came forward, stood in front of the class in a dare-devilish posture. Then he turned his back and drew a life-size picture of a lively warhorse. All his classmates— fifteen boys and ten girls—clapped their hands resoundingly. Derek accepted their applause with a winning smile. His expression indicated that a grand variety entertainment was around the corner.

Derek then announced, 'Class, silence please! From now onwards, all of you must watch breathlessly. First of all, I am going to erase the bushy tail of the horse. What for? Just wait and see! We're going to start the first game.'

Having erased the tail, Derek pointed his finger to an aged figure, made to stand erect behind the class, close to the rear wall. Yes, it was Master Cyril. Master was tightly blindfolded

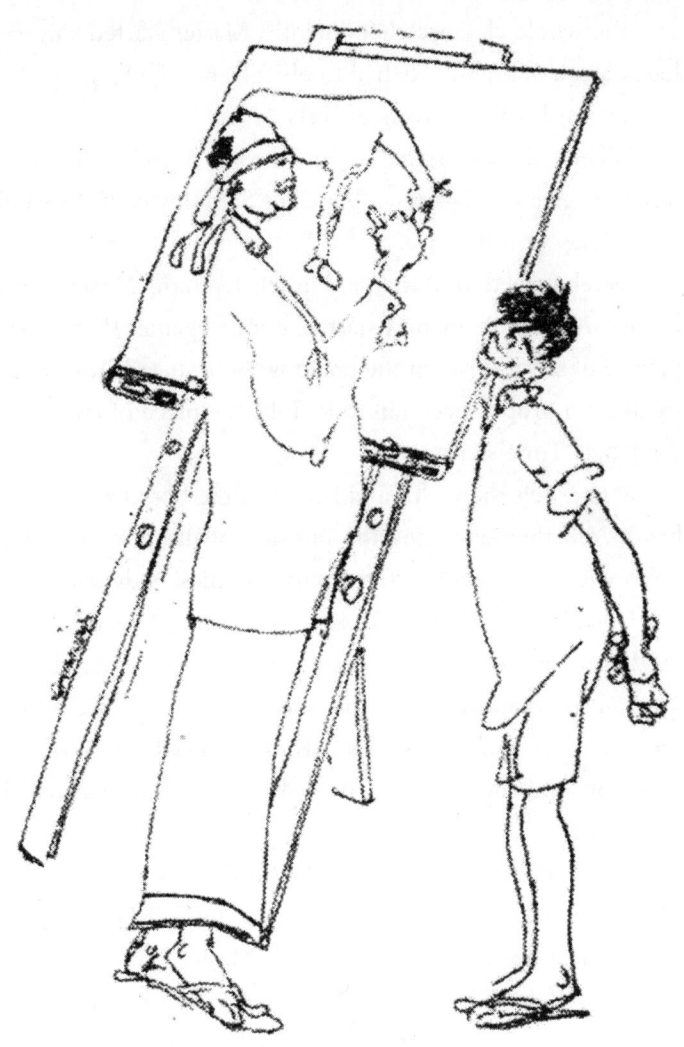

with a thick cloth. Derek commanded, 'Master Cyril, please come to the blackboard which is near me.'

The whole class watched intently. Master started shivering like a leaf in a breeze. He had to obey Derek. So he groped his way forward between rows of seats.

When Master arrived at the board, Derek announced, 'Friends, give our Master a big clap! See, slowly and steadily, Master has won the race.'

Derek turned to Master and instructed him, 'Master, please listen carefully. We are now starting our first game. There is a big picture of a warhorse on the board without its tail. Your task is to attach a proper-sized tail to it. Take the piece of chalk from the ledge. Time starts now!'

Master felt the width and height of the board with his left hand. And then assuming the position of the missing tail, he drew, with a praying heart, that curved, thick body part.

Derek and the whole class shouted. 'Ahoi, Master! What a pity! You have attached the tail to the poor horse's bright eye! The tail has pierced its eye and hurt him severely. See Master, the horse has shaken off all its armour, kicked the board and flown off into the blue sky! What have you done Master? So shameful!'

Derek then removed the blindfold from Master's eyes. Master's face was red and splotchy. He looked like an infant that had just been wailing. Derek said, 'Master, I'll wipe off your tears now!' He did this with the duster which resulted in the creation of two chalky streams on Master's cheeks. The poor man's eyes smarted.

Derek continued, 'Master, we will set you free if you can ask us an intelligent riddle.'

With a wavering voice, Master started. 'My name has five letters. The fifth letter is not after "O" in the alphabet. The organ of movement starts with this letter. My fourth letter is I am myself whereas my first two letters are the same for a mode of conveyance, my last two letters are the same for anti-god. The first, third and second letters of my name form what you do when you are really sad. What is my name?'

Derek shouted, 'Stop Master, stop! Don't bore us! We all know your name! It is Cycle, Devil and Cry all joined together. '

Master's face turned as pale as death.

Then Derek entered the third phase of the agenda. 'Master, listen, you have to repeat this tongue-twister ten times fast. 'Master Monster Baddie Zombie.' A shock wave passed through Master, because he knew those were the epithets conferred on him by the kids. However, he finished the task.

Then Derek announced, 'I'm sure Master will be a sport and happily take part in the next game. Five of us will take turns to be elephant drivers. Master will be the elephant. Each mahout will have two rounds within the class. The bulky ones, Brevard, Betsy, Aaron, Clement and Donald, are chosen for the task. Okay, ready, get, set, go!' Derek blew the whistle. Master soon went on all fours. Carrying the heavy children around was a terribly tedious task. At the end, both his knees felt like rocks. He stood up strenuously.

But then with a tremor of fear, Master heard Derek say, 'We will now switch over to...'

Master dared to interrupt with a lament, 'I feel like going home.'

Derek laughed him down loudly. 'Aww! What a wishful thinking of a nursery kid!'

The whole class burst into laughter.

Derek continued, 'With this item we have to wind up. The name of the game is TREASURE HUNT. No doubt, Master is our treasure. Master will run first into that jungle and hide from us. After five minutes we will enter the jungle and start pelting stones at him. Hitting him is our task. Evading the missiles is left to him. Ready, get, set, go!'

With very heavy legs, Master ran towards the jungle and disappeared. Later, the attacking team chased him. While running, Master could perceive right in front of his eyes, his mangled body bathed in blood! He felt his strength oozing out of his lean legs. In a flash, he saw the faces of his parents and all his preceptors. Stones zoomed past him. He felt that the stones were very considerate to him, and missing him entirely. Suddenly, he changed his line of thought and sobbed. 'In fact, all these stones are directly impinging upon my fragile heart!' He wanted to forget all his pains and worries and go back to his poor, hunch-backed wife who was probably waiting for him with supper in their ancient home. So he mustered all his will and forced his legs to gallop.

But his ruling stars decided otherwise. His legs got frozen and soon he lost sense of location and time. He felt giddy like he was in a whirlpool. In no time, he fell down on the marshy ground and started sweating severely. Sharp thorns pierced and tore his clothes. His limbs and face were bleeding. He lay there desperately. Various scenes appeared before him in a flashback:

When he first entered the school, wearing a student's uniform, the twenty-six letters of the alphabet were written on the blackboard. When he left the school, the letters were still there. Years later, when he came back to the school as a teacher, some of the letters had faded and others were missing. The board yearned to be filled up. And now as he was retiring, pathetically, he found the blackboard to be totally blank, eternally empty. On the ledge of the black board there were heaps of broken buttons from school uniforms and fag-ends of narcotic rolls. The scrolls of knowledge had gone with the wind. Master concluded that his was a lost life, and all the while he had been planting and nursing rosebushes not for their flowers, but for their thorns!

'My name is four-lettered. That is both a salty drop as well as an act to rend something asunder. Do you know my name, do you know my name, do you know my name? My name is, my name is, my name is TEAR.' With deep exhaustion, Master cried for water. Right then a heavy stone hit his chest hard. Derek and party who were chasing him found him in a very desperate condition. They were obliged to meet Master's demand for water. In a jiffy, Master recognized around him the presence of his diabolical disciples.

Derek had now grown devilish horns on his head, and he now had a long tail, a tusk and fiery eyes. Derek took out from his back pocket a bottle, opened it and slowly poured out its contents into Master's mouth. 'Master, here is the drink you wanted. You have to drink the whole lot now. Do not talk. If you talk, your body will get heated up. That will reduce the efficacy. Gradually you will feel heaviness and numbness building up from your legs. And when it reaches your chest…'

Master drank the liquid fully. He continued to lie there. He focused and smiled at a solitary star. Then his eyes dimmed with tears; he sobbed his heart out. 'Now, it's time for me to pass through the tragedy of my life up to its culmination, namely, the death, which is my birthright…'

~

'Yes, Echecritus, such was the end of the most righteous, most virtuous and the wisest man I have ever known in my life.' This was the concluding sentence in the biography of Socrates, as narrated by his disciple Phedo to Echecritus. That sentence resounded in the ears of Master who had just finished reading the book a second time. The book lay on his chest as he slept. Soon Master startled out of his sleep and with a heavy heart, took hold of his teaching notes. But then he lamented, 'Today was my last day at school. No more teaching session for me in the school from tomorrow onwards. Yes, very true, no more classes.'

# 13

## Heads I Win, Tails You Lose!

Pedestrians walk steadily on the highway one sultry afternoon. Two men come from opposite directions and meet at a junction on the highway.

The two men glare at each other ferociously with their bloodshot, round eyes. All on a sudden, in unison, they draw out their long, sharp and glittering knives from their scabbards. The two men's feet now adopt the rigorous steps of martial arts. They shift their feet left and right, left and right. The sharp blades of the two knives graze each other.

After that what can we infer? It is quite simple: anything can happen now! So we reason that things develop very rapidly. Each knife-tip will pierce its rival's throat. There it would make a violent jerk, squirting blood all over the two bodies. Then, from these tremulous bodies, heads would be detached. Thereafter, the two headless trunks would run helter-skelter along the street in two opposite directions.

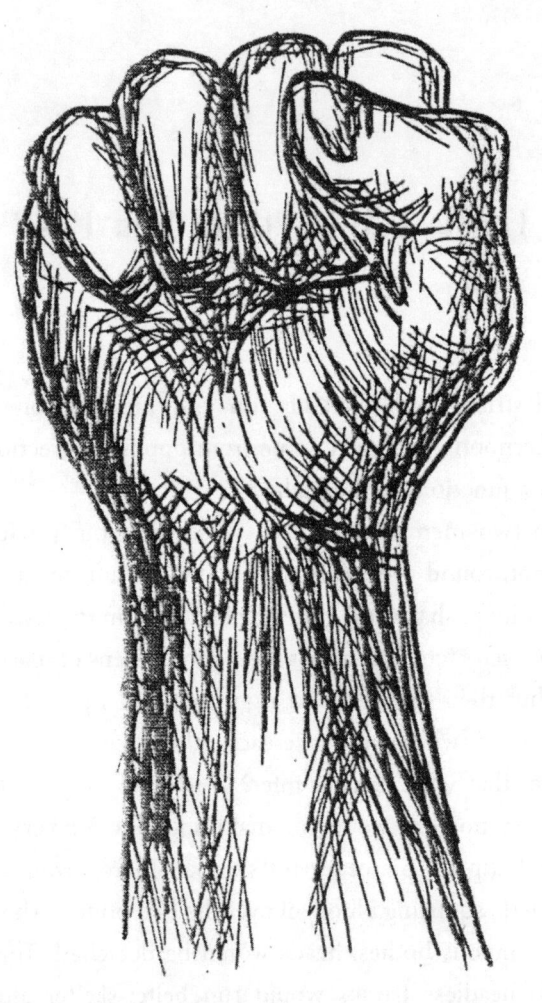

But no, not at all! Nothing of that sort happens here right now.

In the meantime, as if by magic, from either side of the junction, two long processions of people approach the men, shouting wild slogans. The two men who are the leaders of the two groups rejoin their own separate factions. Subsequently, the two groups stand face to face along the road. With fists thrown out into the air, they shout, 'We'll take revenge ourselves. We will take revenge ourselves'

The colour of the flag of one party was crimson while that of the other party was cream. And see, when it comes to their proclaimed manifestos, one can find practically no difference at all between them. Surprisingly, even these two leaders looked like twin brothers; it is very difficult to tell them apart.

For whom are we striving day in and day out? Why are we standing in the hot sun for hours on end? What for are we undertaking the herculean tasks of organizing long processions as well as of maintaining law and order within cadres and factions? Just understand, they are no joke at all! Why, why? Only you have sown and so you have to reap the harvest yourself! Or else, who is there to look after you and your comforts?

~

There is a big hoarding installed in the no man's land between the offices of the two groups.

The writing there reads: Heads I win, Tails you lose!

We bank with VOTEBANK

Voice of the LEADER is the voice of the people.

# 14

## Bindi

A bindi exactly like the fiery solar disc is planted right in the middle of Sulu's forehead. Every morning, as well as every afternoon, after her siesta, Sulu performed this ritual with religious exactitude. Her bindi added charm to her luxuriant hair which flowed down to cover her back.

One afternoon, she heard a knock at the door of her cottage. Who else could that be other than Sonu, her doting husband, a soldier now posted in the war front?

Sulu was staying alone. She was unable to move at a good pace because she was in the advanced stage of pregnancy. The seed sown in her womb about eight months ago had developed deep roots, branches and leaves, and was capable enough to swirl and dance as in a breeze. So Sulu stepped ahead leisurely and answered the door. But she was deeply disappointed. The visitor was a total stranger, a young man. He straightaway started communicating with her through wordless gestures and gesticulations. Sulu made out the gist of what he meant.

He was gesturing to the beautifully carved-out wooden chair beside him. He said that he was a carpenter by trade and had made this piece of furniture in three weeks. He could not run a shop on his own because unscrupulous agents used to cheat him. So now he goes around from door to door trying to sell his products and make a living. Since he was handicapped, people were considerate to him.

As a spontaneous and sympathetic response, Sulu did not speak back, but gestured instead. She asked him how much the chair cost. She gestured that her husband would come home at the end of the month. At the moment, in the house, there were only two stools and an old chair. So it would be a matter of pride to own such a royal chair. But the seller demanded an exorbitant price, not affordable by her. She only had half that amount ready. From her innocent expression, he fully believed it. He changed his tactics. He indicated that as she reminded him of his own sister, he would sell her the chair at her stated price. Sulu handed over the cash and the chair found its place in her house.

A bit reluctantly, she sat in that graceful chair that was meant for her husband and imitated the pose her husband often took. Then she imagined that the chair was linked to a star in the firmament. Slowly, she got drifted into sleep.

The next week on the same day and during the same time, she heard a knock at her door. Her bulging belly moved very slowly. When she opened the door, she was wonderstruck. A police jeep stood outside. Two police officers along with the deaf and dumb carpenter stood at her door. Sulu was feeling terribly dizzy. In order to steady herself, she caught hold of the new chair and leaned against the wall. The chief police officer asked her readily. 'Who else is here?'

Sulu said, 'I am alone here.'

One of the officers replied, 'How is that in this stage you are alone here?'

'I have a domestic help in the morning. And our neighbour, Aunt Mathu comes to stay the night.'

The officer said, 'Well, that's none of my concern. The problem is that you have done two crimes!'

Sulu's mind sank into a melancholy pit. The word 'crime' sent shivers through her spine. Yet, she was quite curious to know about her 'crimes'. The officer stood there with a grave face and said slowly, 'Crime number one: when a young stranger came and knocked at your door, you should not have opened the door for him. There are no provisions here to check on visitors. No peephole, no viewfinder! And no camera! Again, well, that is none of my concern. I am not a social worker either. I am just a representative of the government, an officer assigned to maintain law and order here in this locality.'

The officer's face boiled over with rage. 'Now, over to the second crime. And because of that crime, you have become an offender in accordance with the penal code.'

Just then the baby jumped in her womb as a protest against framing its mother an 'offender'.

'You have secretly and illegally accepted a stolen property, obviously, at a damn cheap price from this thief! And do you know whose chair it is? And how this bastard managed to steal it? He coolly went to the residence of the chief judge, did some odd jobs and then cunningly loosened two legs of this chair. He then carried it out after informing the guard at the gate that it needed urgent repairs! You know that the judge is from the erstwhile ruling family, and the chair was a throne! And you know how we nabbed him? In the nearby village pond, a young lady was taking her bath. This rogue approached her with his vulgar slang and gestures. Listening to her loud screams, her brother came running out and swooped down on him. Luckily, it so happened that the brother was the judge's guard. See, how wonderfully justice is revealed! This guard was about to lose his job! You forgot to notice one thing. He acted dumb and deaf before you and he spoke obscene language to that lady!' The officer hit the thief in the head and asked him to pronounce his name, which he did!

Noticing the hullabaloo next door, Aunt Mathu rushed in. Sulu told Mathu about what she had been accused with. Mathu pleaded with the officer. 'Sir, you know, she is eight months gone with child! Her husband is a soldier in the Border Security Force. If something happens to her, the government will hold you responsible. All womenfolk here buy from street vendors. In this stage, Sulu cannot go out alone to buy a chair. So if this man sold her a chair, do you mean to say she should have asked him for the production certificate? It is sheer nonsense!' Aunt Mathu thrust two fresh banknotes into the police officer's hands. 'So, Sir, I suggest you to bend your rule. Buying stolen property may be an offence. So take your police diary and write, "The stolen royal chair was retrieved from the thief's residence."

That closes the chapter forever. The more you stand here, the more troublesome it is to the child. So please take the chair and clear the scene.'

The police officer listened to Aunt Mathu's advice and rode away in the police jeep. For the first time in her life, Sulu did not care to mend her bindi which had been disrupted by her tensed up fingers. She heaved a deep, sad sigh. 'One, we lost a good amount of money unnecessarily. Two, I had my first experience of police harassment. Three, Sonu doesn't have the royal luck to sit in a royal chair! Four, O, Lord God, why is it that some people feign dumb and deaf just to make normal people like me dumb and deaf?

Sulu's fiery bindi remained disrupted. She was unable to come back to her normal state.

# 15

# Two Sons

Once upon a time there lived a man who had two sons named Sky-Viewer and Mind-Viewer. The nomenclature modus operandi was not a mere childish exercise. As soon as a child was born, Father would note down the precise time and geographical location of the child's birth. Then he would rush to an astrologer and come back with the child's detailed horoscope. Father was adept at analysing and reading the implied meanings of the horoscope. He used to sit in a closed room, place his hands on the horoscope, close his eyes, meditate, chant hymns and pray for a full thirty minutes. Then he would open his eyes and search for the profound meanings and guidelines to arrive at the choicest name with due consideration to the infant's attitude and aptitude.

Sky-Viewer walked always looking upward to the sky. He knew everything about the various constellations, stars, nebula, eclipses, meteors and effects of seasonal changes occurring in the sky. His head was always lifted up and his eyes were always

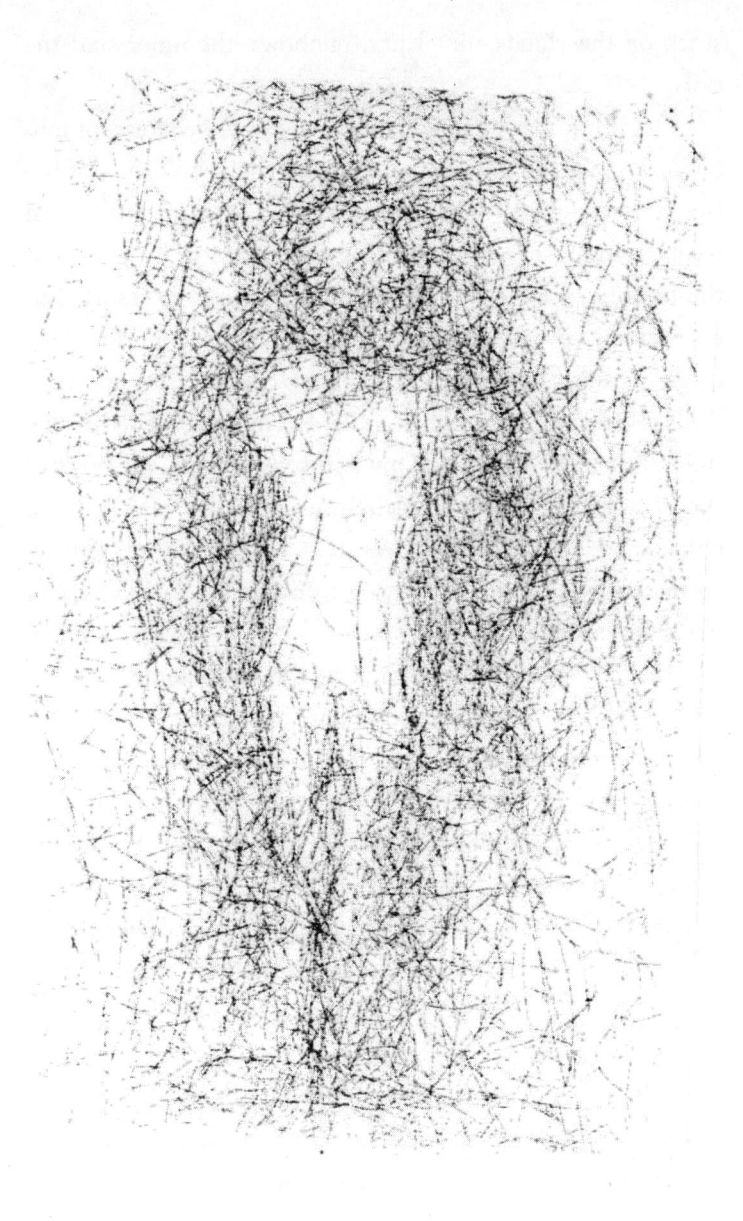

stuck on the clouds, air planes, rainbows, the moon and the stars.

The Mind-Viewer wouldn't look anywhere else except into his own inner self. The entirely different temperaments of the two boys set many tongues wagging. Father heard of this and wept profusely. He tried changing the nature of his sons, but the boys were adamant and unchanging. He even resorted to conjuration, invocation, incantation, sorcery, witchcraft, black magic, casting of mystic spells on them, crystal gazing and tarot cards. He found these things futile. He then pleaded with the ruling planets. 'Please make my two sons HOME-VIEWERS!' But that prayer did not reach heaven. So his tales of woe remained. He asked himself, 'Am I an accursed father?' Finally he understood the folly of trying to overcome the dictates of the ruling planets.

The Sky-Viewer went on viewing the sky. One time he was knocked down by a vehicle, another time a buffalo charged at him. One evening he fell into a pond, and another young girl rescued him. The worst case was when he stared at the solar eclipse for its entire duration and lost his eyesight! Helplessly, Father cried bitterly.

The Mind-Viewer always sat in his study and viewed his own mind. After many years, father heard him reciting his own poem. 'The boy who had left his home, has now come back/ The man who went to lie in the cemetery has now returned to his mother's womb/When I view deep into my mind/ I see the whole Universe reflected there. /Because ultimately everything converges into my psyche/ which is the essence of the Universe.'

Father peeped into his room. His son was sporting a long beard. His hair was matted and there was now a bulging third eye on his forehead. Father knew his son had become a poet. 'But if he is an unacknowledged legislator of the world, he must come out.'

Father reflected. A senior poet after reading the boy's brilliant poem wept because he knew the boy would die soon, as the earth can't contain a super genius for long. Once a Zen Buddhist had asked Father to discover his own two faces. The one before his birth and the one after his death. 'Then you will know your present face is unreal.' Father looked into the mirror to see his unreal face but he saw there the faces of his two sons!

# 16

## Mark in the Dark

Mark stretched himself calm and straight on the floor of the living room and murmured with humility, 'I apologize, I apologize, I apologize for all my ancestors.' Right then, Mark saw a yellow soul flying across the grey horizon. In its wide open eyes, Mark perceived red, burning embers. An owl sitting on the window sill hooted. Mark contemplated, tomorrow somebody may ask me, 'O, Mark O, Mark, whatever has happened to you?' Then I could very well say, 'The stains of the history of sins of my forefathers and the skeletons from the attic are getting dumped into the hollow of my truncated skull.' But no, I won't say that truth. Instead of that my reply will be, 'I don't know anything, I don't know anything.'

While lying, Mark visualized the angelic, cherubic face of Loretta, his eight-year-old daughter. She asked with a worried look, 'Papa, Papa, something wrong with you? Why your face is twisted from fright?'

Mark replied, 'Nothing dear, nothing. If you come here, we

can play Blind Man's Bluff, Hit and Run, Snakes and Ladders or another of your school games. Or we can build a playhouse or play on the swing. But I will never tell you stories because the stories of my ancestors have spoiled my world and my mood. So if possible, never lend your ear to my stories. If you hear them, then you will miss three things: peace of mind, the smile of cool moonlight and the happy friendship of the world. In its place you will get three things: fright, fright, fright. So dear daughter, don't see stories, don't tell stories, don't listen to stories. They'll damage your whole life. You always keep stories at a distance. You move away from their path. I am telling you this because of my own experiences.'

Forty-four-year-old Mark comes back alone to his ancestral home in the village after twenty years of expatriation. He is the sole heir to that vast land and the house, which is surrounded by a high and strong compound wall. A caretaker, Jonathan, was appointed long back. Mark came to know later that Jonathan had spread the news that he had purchased the land and the house from its owners. So far Mark has got no revenue from that plot. Mark's father sold more than nine-tenth of the vast estate to three or four parties some five years ago. It was something like a premonition because within one month after the execution of the sale Mark's father died in a car accident. At that time Mark could not come because he had been hospitalized for two months with jaundice. Mark's wife is German. She doesn't want to visit his native land. They have two daughters. The elder one, Lynda, is fourteen.

Mark's visit surprises Jonathan. Mark's great great

grandfather was the right hand man of the then ruler of that vast locality. He had acquired the property while working for the erstwhile ruler. Under him there were ten families of peasants. In all, Mark's ancestor had hired about a hundred daily workers to work in his estates and farms. He controlled everything like a dictator.

Up to the age of seven, Mark grew up in that house with his grandmother. After that he went to live with his father, who was working abroad. He wanted to make a mark in the world.

Mark learnt all the stories about his ancestral home from his aged grandmother who was a great fan of the patriarch, her dictator father-in-law. Grandma would put on the garb of the wife of a great warlord. She drew a clean sketch of that veteran feudal lord. She filled that sketch with the deep red colour of red-hot fire and fresh blood. That sketch reeked of aristocracy and snobbishness.

The horrible thriller stories she told Mark as bedtime tales, in fact, illustrated the hellish nature of the ancient domestic abode where he resided.

In the night, little Mark would imagine that there was a wrestler-like murderer standing near the back door with a sharp knife. Once there had been such a murderer who had tried to take the patriarch's life. He had been overpowered and thrown into the Death Well. On many nights Mark felt like he heard the heart-rending wails of those souls from that notorious well. Many, many such 'disobedient' souls were thrown alive into that deathly well.

Many supervisors also used to tell Little Mark tales of the

adventures of the great old masters of his 'noble, aristocratic' family!

Later, while sitting alone, Mark imagined that he was listening to the incessant wailings from the outhouse of defiled wombs, wailings of shoe flower-like embryos trampled down mercilessly, and the wails of wriggling and writhing tender orphan girls. Mark also witnessed the loud sobs of a niece of marriageable age as she committed suicide by hanging herself from a branch of the mango tree facing the patriarch's window. The patriarch had rejected her lover.

Mark has now come back with the intention of selling his ancestral house and property. Mark says, 'I am here alive. So the question of intestacy does not arise at all. So why am I being intimidated? Why are people looking to tear me into pieces and take hold of my assets?'

Dry-looking green lichen plants covered the estate's ancient walls and tree-trunks! On the walls of the living room black and white pictures of all his ancestors are hung. Mark had a vision that all these pictures were falling down onto him one after the other and hurting him. Slowly a drizzle formed on the edges of his eyelashes. He saw a line of headless trunks in front of him, dancing. Then Mark said to himself, 'This is the history lesson my ancestral home is teaching me. Heart-rending cries from the death-well, a garland of skulls hung in the attic…'

Grandma once told Mark, 'My dear grandson, remember that the prestige and grandeur of a family cannot be purchased. It is handed down to patriarchs of each generation, and every one of them strives hard to maintain it, safeguard it.'

Mark had a vision:

Grandma now urges him, the latest patriarch to rise to the occasion. Mark replies, 'I'm sorry Grandma. I do not want to have any share of this ferocious heritage. I will not attach the family's insignia on the archaic ancestral blazer...'

# 17

# Welcome to the Finale

It is the final day of the golden jubilee celebration of the prestigious Women's Club. There have been college and school level competitions in literature, elocution, dance, music, mimicry, painting and drama. More than thirty institutions have participated. Advance registration is necessary for these competitions. Expert judges are brought in. Big business houses are sponsors who offered expensive prizes.

The final two competitions are to be held today. For these, on-the-spot entry is admissible. One is the smiling competition for kids aged below six years. And the other is the eating competition. Their flagship competition was announced three months ago through visual and print media in a very catchy style. The competition is for skilled or unskilled workers of the country who work for the maximum number of hours in a day. The time of travel to the place of work and back can also be included. Detailed applications with authorized supportive documents are duly received and a judging committee chose

the winner. The winner, Mr Augustine, is invited to be present to receive the felicitation and the prize. Today being Sunday, he is free to attend. He has come alone, three hours before the ceremony. The volunteers received Augustine and offered him a special seat temporarily in a corner of the platform. The big hall is fully air-conditioned and extensively decorated. He witnessed the thirty-minute smiling competition and then the thirty-minute eating competition. During the smiling competition, ten kids come one after the other and perform for two minutes.

Augustine watches the training being imparted by each mother to her ward. One mother tells her son, 'My dear son, just look at my face. You smile like this, without twisting your face. Your smile must be happy and beautiful. Don't be shy when you look at the people sitting in front of you. Don't pull a face.'

'Mom, I cannot sneeze without closing my eyes. I cannot smile without seeing or listening to something funny. In my cursive writing book, it is written, "No Cheating While You Smile." Simply smiling at serious people is bad manners.'

'Son, what is in your book, let it lie there only. Now don't think of anything else. Simply smile like an angel. Now, look at that child there. His smile is excellent. You have to smile better than that if you want the first prize.'

'Mom, what's wrong with you? He's not smiling, he's going to weep!'

Augustine felt that it was all snobbery. He left the seat and went to where six eating competitors were seated. One wrestler, two athletes, a coast guard, a school physical trainer and a pale-looking tribal youth were talking to each other. Someone commented in a low voice, 'This guy has come not to compete. He wants only free food.'

Augustine took pity on him. He went and talked to that young man. The man had wrapped a banner of a political party around his stomach to cover the area where his shirt was torn. He is Rangan. Since it was raining last week, he did not get any manual work. He is an orphan. No work means no money and no food. 'In the morning, I joined a political party's procession and they gave me some money. With that money I was going to eat something. Then I heard that here is an eating competition. To eat maximum, I didn't take in anything; only a little pipe-water. I am very tired. I hope I will not faint,' Rangan said.

'You think about winning only. I wish you the best luck. You keep on smiling at yourself only,' Augustine replied.

Then the announcement came: 'The eating competition is about to start now. A truckload of idlis is available. We request the viewers to avoid supporting individual competitors because that will disturb the peaceful atmosphere. Thank you all.'

Vertical boards are placed between the competitors. They cannot see one another. Twelve judges look on. Viewers are able to see the complete competition. Augustine stood watching Rangan's involvement. Rangan has his own technique. His is a strange strategy. He pulverizes the idlis, mixes the chutney and consumes the good. So he is far ahead of the other competitors. Augustine rejoices.

But what a pity! Poor Rangan! His weak intestines are not habituated to eating a full stomach, let alone to overeating. Alas, he faints! The organizers take him in an ambulance to the hospital. Augustine sheds a tear.

It was almost time to start the meeting. A lady volunteer comes to Augustine, and fixes a rose flower on his shirt and sprays a perfume on him lavishly. He is led along the red carpet to his reserved seat on the platform.

The master of the ceremony announces, 'Ladies and gentlemen, we are now presenting Mr Augustine Fernandez, as the winner of the widely popular "Mister Hercules of the year" contest. He leaves home at 4 a.m. with his lunch box to reach the railway station that is 10 kilometres away on his bicycle. He takes the train to the city where he is welder in a factory. At 5 p.m. he leaves and goes to work in another factory as a welder. He goes home at 9 p.m. He has two brilliant college-going children. His wife is a homemaker. His aged parents have been bedridden for about ten years. His father had a thriving business, but his business partner, a litigious person, cheated him. He became paralytic. His only son sacrificed his ambition of entering the Civil Services to study welding. By the time Augustine reaches home it is after midnight. He sees the smiling faces of his children only on Sundays.

(Listening to this, Augustine was not at all feeling proud and comfortable.)

'Now I kindly invite to the dais our chief guest Ms Brenda Clara Charles and Ms Mili Tara, the President of the Women's Club. Thank you all.'

Augustine felt quite uneasy on the dais, like a fish out of water. The chief guest, with all her make-up looked glamorous.

She started her speech. 'Dear friends, first of all I want to divulge an important information to you. In college, Mr Augustine was my senior, and our college union chairman. He was a versatile genius and a firebrand orator. I am not sure whether he remembers me. He was reputed to be the most eligible and the most handsome bachelor of our college. His perfect manners produced a very formidable impression on all…'

A sudden flash opened up Augustine's memory bank and left him rattled. His mind flew back to perch on a campus tree. It was the night of the Youth Festival. Augustine heard whispers in the dimly lit backyard. A minicar was also parked there. 'Dev, I am really afraid, please leave me alone. This will become a scandal tonight itself. My daddy will shoot me on the spot.'

'My honey, don't be a coward. This is the only golden opportunity for us. I'll drop you back within half an hour. Don't worry, dear. We'll take all the precautions. Please come…'his voice trails.

'Oh my darling, I was just kidding. I simply wanted to test you.'

Augustine jumps in wildly. He catches hold of the girl's hand firmly and shouts, 'Go back now itself. Although not good at studies, you're very good at these things! And you, you silly girl, you don't know this rich scoundrel. He is a bull; he has spoiled a dozen girls. Don't be a blood-sucking seductress. Return now! And I'll keep this a secret.'

Back to the dais. Augustine felt terribly weak. He didn't want to receive the award from her. He levitated. Soon a ball of fire emerged out of his eyes and burnt down the dais, the hall, including his prospective shield.

# 18

# Hey, There

'Hey, there! Just halt!'

The words sent cold shivers down my back. I started perspiring. Beads of sweat emerged on my forehead, chest and armpits. The bundle of many, very important loose papers slipped from my hand. I stamped on the scattered papers to prevent them from flying off. Could I collect all? I'm not sure. If it's lost, it is! I stood up and looked at the man in front of me with a questioning gaze. He had a crooked face!

He shouts at me, 'Where's the money you've snatched from Kevin's chest of drawers? He had withdrawn the money from the bank for his wife's treatment. We searched all the people who were present in the room, but in vain. You were the first to leave the office. And you escaped!'

'What nonsense are you talking? You've no right to intimidate me like this!'

'Yes, you can do nonsense, but I should not question you! You don't know Kevin's true colours and his links with higher ups! If you want to see the light of tomorrow, return him the money soon.'

'Hey, there! Just halt!'

Beads of sweat emerged on my body.

'See, this is my girlfriend. I admit that the bus was crowded. That doesn't mean you can misbehave with my girl! You don't know my real nature! I'll teach you a lesson to last for your whole life, indeed!'

'What are you driving at? While standing in the bus, both my hands were holding on to the central bar!'

'Oh, this is the greatest joke of the year! By your statement you are claiming that you have four hands, just like a goddess.'

'Hey, there! Just halt!'

Beads of sweat emerged on my body...

'Whose signature is this?'

'That's mine.'

'You put this signature?'

'Let me see the paper closely. Someone else has forged my signature. I don't have to pay this much money to somebody. Don't come up with false allegations. I'm not a party to this agreement!

'That part you simply leave to me! I think you want to breathe properly. If so, better, make arrangements to pay the money to the person concerned!'

'Hey, there! Just halt!'

Beads of sweat appeared on my body...

'Who was that lady? What was the dispute? A jilted love affair? Illicit pregnancy? Dowry-demands? Family-dissents?

Extramarital affairs? Property partition disputes? Tell me, tell me frankly. What was the reason?'

'About that woman. I have not even a nodding acquaintance with her.'

'Don't bluff, don't lie to me. There is strong evidence against you! Otherwise why are we here as guardians of law and order! There's no other go! You are under arrest for the murder of that innocent woman!'

'Hey, there! Just halt!'

Oh, whatever on earth is happening here! The words send cold shivers down my back.

I start perspiring. Beads of sweat emerge on my forehead, chest and armpits.

Oh, enough, enough! I can't stand it any longer!

Here, I go off into a F-A-I-N-T!

# 19

## The Story Recitation

In the mini hall, in front of the audience, the writer read out his entire short story in ten minutes, with proper pauses, stresses and varying intonation.

'Great!' 'Marvellous!' 'Brillant!' The writer won the applause of the audience.

But the chairman dissented rudely. 'There are many flaws in the composition of the story. All of your clapping should have instead been planted on the writer's cheeks!'

The audience resented the criticism. 'Will you please explain the reasons?'

The chairman read out a sentence and then a paragraph of the story. After that he commented, 'This is a clear-cut example of the writer's animal passions getting an incarnation. A true sublimation!'

The audience cried out, 'What about that sentence you have read out?'

'That sentence! It totally spoils the spirit of the story. Simply

do away with it.'

'And what about that paragraph?'

'See, in the story, the innocent hero is imprisoned unjustly because the jury had accepted false witnesses. And naturally, his wife is driven almost insane due to her unbearable grief. The story should delineate her current mindset in this fashion: "A nightingale perched on the weeping willow at the jail-gate resounded a profound wail. She said, 'Whatever I sang were not songs at all. Whatever I hummed were not tunes at all! And my permanent abode is the tent of pitch darkness.' Listening to this wail, a male soul behind the prison bars flew to her. He touched her in the form of a gloomy pulse and a melancholic fiery drop. Right then another male figure fled from his dark hideout. Soon her cry was heard. 'I won't come with you; I won't throw away my nuptial string. No, no, no!'

The soul that arrived now heaved a sigh of relief."'

The audience applauded again. What a joke! The chairman who pointed out the flaws of the story critically was none other than the story writer himself! When the assembly congratulated him, a boy posed a question, 'Then why didn't you think of those slips before finishing the story?'

The story writer retorted with a smile, 'My dear boy, if I had done so, then as Chairman of the Literary Club, what role will I play here? Moreover, remember that the only thing which doesn't change is change itself. So why can't the story change too?'

'After all, a story starts at a pinpoint as a river begins its life as a trickle at a mountain-top,' said the chairman.

It was time for the writer to startle out of his sleep.

# 20

## Quite Near, Yet Quite Far

My evening walk that day took me to the side of a community hall where some sort of a celebration was being held. The loudspeaker blared out a series of old and new film songs. There were full-blown rain-clouds in the sky. Like the air, my mind was also gloomy. The meaning of the song was this, 'Up to the house, the kith and kin; up to the road the better half, and up to the crematorium the sons: but who'll be there up to the end?' The song spoke about the dead body of the master of the house, and how his wife was not permitted to go to the crematorium.

It was only three months ago that I purchased a new house in the heart of the city. So I have not started to make friends with my neighbours and other local residents. During my wakeful hours I like to write. So I am very choosy about my associations.

Recently, I wrote a novelette and sent it to a leading literary journal for publication. A fortnight later, I received a message

from the editor asking for a large colour-photo of mine.

I entered a photo studio, named Image Plus, which was located at the triangular junction of two main roads. A semicircular board with a multi-coloured illustration was put up on the entrance of the studio which did not seem too busy.

Job, the photographer, made a good impression on me. He seemed like a mature youngster. I told him about my requirement.

A photographer, being a sensitive artist, might have developed a soft spot towards a novelist. Job insisted I drink a cup of Nescafe, which he poured out, from his flask. Evening cups of coffee used to give me disturbed sleep. But as it was our first meeting, I did not refuse it.

The next evening, he presented me with an appealing picture of mine with a comment. He said, 'Taking photographs of photogenic people is highly satisfactory.'

I laughed loudly and remarked, 'Job, when you say that, I conclude, you've unrealistically made me over smart.'

Job put on a long face and said, 'Sir, I did not mean so.'

I patted him and said, 'Forget it, I was just joking.'

While taking leave of him, he said that he would be honoured if I could sit with him on some evenings. He added that all his neighbours were pretending to be very busy and he had no company. I agreed on one condition: 'No coffee, tea or cigarettes!' From my many sessions with him, I noted with amazement that he kept abreast of international current affairs and politics. I was most surprised when he showed me his paintings arranged in a small room in the studio. I then remembered a simile about a painting that I had read in an ancient book, the Vishnudharma epic. It said that a painting is like the Himalayas among the arts, the bird-vehicle of Lord Vishnu among birds and the emperor among men.

I noticed that Job's paintings showed scenes of pathos and compassion. They charmed the viewer with graceful symbolic representations and suggestive meanings. A critic will be convinced of the gravity and intellectual honesty emerging from the canvas of this sensitive, artistic mind.

Job said he had to build up more confidence to hold an exhibition. He had not titled any of his paintings because he did not want to interfere with the viewer's perception of them.

There was a painting in which lava flowed down from a red-hot solar disc, into a vast grain field. To me it indicated the atrocities felt in the facts of life. There was a painting about the blood and tears of war. Next was the fiery dance of DEATH, with a heart-rending wild cry: a metaphor of intimidating outrage upon the sense of justice. A graphic etching and a terracotta statue and watercolours and oil paintings were also available. The influence of symbolism and surrealism was evident in all of Job's works.

In our next meeting, Job was holding the weekly, which had published the first part of my novella and my photo taken by him. He said that he liked the first part of the story very much and judging from my nature, the protagonist resembled me!

I said, 'Job, it is too early to jump to conclusions. There is what is called denouement. So don't shoot into the gun. Job, I prefer to write satire that will not mirror the society as such.

Human emotions and sentiments are my top priorities. So just wait and see.'

In our next meeting, Job urgently sought my help for his close friend Sebastian who had a family problem. I told him frankly, 'Job, I'm not a social doctor to cure anyone's domestic illness. When I want to convey something to society through fiction, I create an ambience, characters, events and conflicts to build suspense and readability and above all a good plot. So don't expect a good remedy from me. I can only try.'

'I'm really sorry for troubling you. But my friend is forcing me too much. Please let me tell you my friend's case briefly.'

I gave him the green signal.

Job and Sebastian were from the same village. Job's father was a primary school headmaster and Sebastian's father a farmer. Both were highly respected community leaders. Although a graduate, Sebastian was unable to leave his home to seek a good job faraway. He had a younger sister to be married off and had to take care of the farmland.

Soon his aged parents fell ill. So he joined the rural bank in his village. Taking loans, he conducted his sister's wedding. But with rising domestic expenses and expensive medicines and treatment for his parents, Sebastian was shedding bloody tears. Meanwhile, a client in the bank came up with a marriage proposal. Susan was an undergraduate from a rich family in the city. Sebastian agreed and in due course, a daughter and a son were born to them. Now the daughter, Martha, is fourteen. Sebastian is a calm and quiet chap, humble and peace-loving. On the contrary, Susan is oversmart and liberal. Because of her insistence, Sebastian had to move away from his parents. They are being looked after by a home-nurse. Susan complains about Sebastian's low salary and his inability to make extra money. The situation has reached a critical stage: their mutual communication has come to a standstill. The couple has started sleeping in separate rooms.

In the very middle of one night, he found her talking coquettishly on the phone for half an hour. He didn't question her. But her conversations continued for one week and he reported this to her simple parents. They became terribly upset. Her father told Sebastian, 'Son, I am weak to resolve this problem. I will call my younger brother Vincent. You can go back. I will let you know soon.'

Everybody knows that Vincent is boastful, rude and foulmouthed. He is in the real estate business.

Vincent came in his car with his wife Ruth 'to sort out an urgent family matter'. After the discussion, Ruth said, 'I knew about this from Martha two days ago. I consoled her and said that I will solve this and that she should keep quiet for the good of our family. Martha told me that Susan's friend is Sam. Yesterday Sam's wife called Martha and sobbingly requested her to control Susan. I didn't tell Vincent this because he is short-tempered and would have made a scene, which will publicize the whole matter.'

Vincent replied, 'Ruth, now you call Susan and ask her to come here soon. Tell her that her mother is seriously ill and that's why you are here. Send her the car. She should not bring the children now.'

Susan came in the car. Actually her mother had developed high blood pressure. Vincent asked Susan about the affair. Susan was an entirely changed person. She reacted like a growling tigress.

'When I was immature, you forced a simpleton husband of mine on me. A low-salaried man with no ability to make extra income. Are you jealous that I'm making some good money for me and my children through money chain projects? I'm talking to Sam only about our business matters and he is free only at night. I know Sam's wife is also suspicious. But I cannot help it. This is my personal matter. I'm leaving. I don't need your car,' Susan rushed back haughtily.

Job was panting when he finished his narration. I deliberately posed as a patient listener, only nodding in between. I told Job, 'Job, these days a lot of Facebook elopements, cybercrimes, murders, human trafficking fill the news. A financially independent housewife's tendency is to dominate. Neither counselling, nor family court can help. Later, if Susan becomes totally isolated from her friends and family, she may attempt suicide. That's a bleak picture! I can only wish Sebastian peace of mind. Bye now, Job.'

After this meeting, on the third day, I was informed that my mother was in the intensive care unit in the capital city with my brother. I got there by plane. I had to be there for a month. She recovered fully, thanks to specialist doctors and sophisticated equipment as well as her own willpower.

The evening after my arrival I thought of meeting Job. In the beginning of this narration I hinted about the gloomy day and my gloomy mind. Now the mist is removed sadly. Within thick black borders, under the big caption of Obituary, there was a large portrait of a young man with dreamy, artistic eyes. The frame was garlanded behind the portrait. The semicircular glass door of the studio was locked. No familiar faces around. Other shops also were closed. With folded hands and tearful eyes, I stood there silently for ten minutes.

I was highly curious and anxious to know the reason behind this untimely demise. I telephoned our common friend, the police inspector who was on an official tour with his bosses. He said briefly and in a hurry that Job's wife, a so-called society-lady, had had a secret love-affair with her business partner, a notorious womanizer. All members of the family objected to this relationship. But she was obstinate and strong-willed. A highly sensitive, artistic person, Job was unable to digest this mental shock.

# 21

## Superhuman

### Travel

He had never seen the rubber globe of earth near the side entrance of the shopping mall before. Later, he found that there were similar ones near the main entrance as well as at the exit point. But he did not like to go there. Those places were always very crowded. He christened the globe his 'magic planet'. Soon after the mall opened, he will stealthily enter it and go up to the globe perched on a stand close to the globe. Then he would secretly rotate it slightly and then touch, smell and closely observe the mountains, seas, volcanoes, forests, lakes, the polar regions, locations of monumental high-rise buildings, great bridges, waterfalls, railway lines, wild life sanctuaries, zoos, big market places and malls and tourist resorts. Very slowly, he developed so much insight that he could now even smell and touch elements in various gardens, lakes, snow-clad mountains, coral reefs that the globe depicted. He would imbibe the various types of intoxicating natural fragrances including the smell of the pollen, wet decaying leaves, barks of trees, the soothing smell of brooks, the droppings of large birds, dung of zebras, elephants and kangaroos and the musk of a musk deer.

Ultimately, he made an elaborate plan. He identified various places he would visit. His exhilaration knew no limit. He was highly satisfied with the perfection of his travel agenda. Before going back to his abode for the night, he quite contentedly rotated and kissed the globe once again with his long, grey-tinged beak. Why can't a bird go globetrotting?

~

## See, he is right behind me

He was right behind me! So I ran. But he was determined to catch hold of me. No friend, I won't let you touch me! While running, I consoled myself with the fact that I was carrying a knife, so the monster can't attack me. Then an inner voice commented, 'That all depends on how fast you run!

When I looked back hurriedly, I noticed that his left and right hands and legs were not moving in coordination! For a moment, I imagined that he was riding on a giant wind with a super speed.

Hurrah! I have won the competition with a photo finish! My willpower and stamina helped me defeat him. I stepped on my porch with shouts of joy!

So he could not attack and drench me at all. He, yes, is the rain!

~

## She

Oh, my honey, I very much appreciate your promptness in reporting to me every day in the morning! But darling, I'm very tired now because after a long trip I came home late last night. So I forgot to pull down the window shade. I'm alone here, so is it not pardonable?

After my late arrival, as my eyelids were heavy with sleep, I rushed to embrace my bed and pillow! Listlessly, I slept.

My dear lassie, I thank you very much for lying with me and giving me company. I note that you enjoy my romantic prattle! I'm still sleepy. So let me sleep for two more hours!

Oh, it is eleven in the morning! Still you're sleeping with me, your warm hands holding on to me tightly! Oh girl, you make my bare body abnormally hot! Sorry, now you get up and go out! I'll pull down the window shade. Bye my dear sunlight!

## 22

# Under a Vow

James was standing in an art gallery and staring fixedly at the portrait of a slim damsel, appreciating her feminine charm, grace and figure. She was stark naked except for three olive leaves covering three strategic points of her sexy constitution.

Right then, Treesa, his fiancée silently appeared behind him and took him by surprise. She embraced him and asked him with jubilation, 'My sweetheart, are you waiting for the leaf-shedding season?'

James blushed. Before their wedding he used to jeer at her by labelling her as a wet painting, which required time to mature! But when she resisted, he retorted that she was to him what oxygen was to fire. He subsequently tickled her in her ribs. That culminated in an endearing kiss and Treesa was particularly ticklish.

Yes, those were the days before their marriage.

But now that many months have passed since their marriage. In the glass of milk which she had served him, James sees the

head of a small lizard. When he points this out to Treesa, she tells him, 'Oh, James, I had dropped it there to catch the housefly in the milk.'

James remembered one of his boyhood incidents. His mom held his hand, crossed the snowy meadow, passed the mangroves and marigold plants and finally reached the cemetery where among the departed souls his Papa was lying. James now entertains a tender dream that his Papa would revive and come up to embrace him and Mom.

Mom was wailing. 'My son, when your Papa died, he was keeping perfect health. In fact, the departure happened all of a sudden. My son, after that, I too was dead. I lost all my energies. The future was totally dark.'

'Mom, Mom…' James weeps.

'Yes my son. I was no more…' Mom sobbed heavily. Before his twenty-fifth birthday James received a letter from Mom. She had written it very slowly with a shivering hand, from her sick bed. A home-nurse was taking care of her. James, Treesa, Treesa's parents, her two brothers and their families lived in the same locality, but each family was independent. Mom wrote: 'My dear son, your twenty-fifth birthday is approaching. Please don't forget your Mom's vow. Please don't make the saints angry.'

After reading that letter James underwent a terrible emotional shock. He sat there alone for a long time. Then James recollected Mom's old utterances.

When James was seven, Mom related her first dream to James. 'Son, listen. Some snow-white hands pushed a silver platter towards me. I plucked a fully blossomed and beautiful red flower and placed it with awe and respect on the platter along with the flowers of my tears. Gradually that red flower transformed itself into your body. Then I was terribly shocked. I went on beating my chest and sobbing non-stop. I saw you on the sickbed like a pale stick. You stared at me. I scooped you up and hugged you with all my heart.'

James was now drifting into a dream. It was a nightmarish affair. There was a long, narrow and dark cave. It looked never-ending. He thought he saw a light at the end of the tunnel, but wasn't sure. Still he proceeded further, hoping against hope. He walked on and on, earnestly praying for at least a spark of light there. On the way he heard thunderous shouts. Those harsh sounds were impinging very hard on his eardrums. Just then he recognized that familiar voice of his own blood. It was his mother: 'My dear son, I am telling you again and again, you must know who you are. You must know how you have grown up and reached this stage. Many years ago, when you were just a slip of a boy, your whole body was inflicted with leprosy-type red sores emitting thick, yellow, smelly puss. In that puss very minute worms wriggled. You were also wailing and writhing with excruciating pain. Do you know who saved you? Do you know who saved your life?'

Her voice continued to shout. 'My dear son, the very body of yours which you are embellishing with sophisticated perfumes, the very body of yours which you are exhibiting to the whole world, was once totally rejected by all medications, all treatments, all hospitals and all doctors. This happened exactly one month after I had that dream of the silver platter and red flower. I was helplessly crying my heart out. Then I offered your body to the saints. That was my last hope. I cringed and grovelled before them and thus borrowed your dear life from them. We owe your life entirely to them. As a gesture of gratitude to those divine souls, my dear son, I had given my word to those saints. I have told you that story before. And now, that occasion has come. I am only reminding you. Don't neglect this vow of mine. Otherwise, we will have to swallow the wrath of the saints. And it will be a horrible, unbearable, hellish experience! Again I say this letter is only a strong reminder to you. Your remaining life is absolutely at their divine mercy. We are obliged to them. We are totally indebted to them. Your very life was saved by a miracle.'

James travelled back the memory lane.

In the dead of the night, when he was seven, he twisted and turned on his bed with high temperature. His red eyes rolled into the back of his head. Soon he became delirious. He started muttering wildly. His body felt like a hot kiln. Mom passed her slender fingers over his pulsating ribs and threw her quivering head up to heaven and cried aloud, 'My respected, venerable holy saints, I'll do anything you want, but please save my young son's life. After his twenty-fifth birthday, within a month, I will see to it that he will visit forty houses as a beggar, with a begging bowl and receive alms from those houses.'

And today is that red-letter day. His twenty-fifth birthday.

Suddenly, James imagined a luxury bus coming down a steep hill, skidding off the track and falling into a chasm! It was a hallucination.

In his mind, James had a vivid picture of his future scenario. He would hear an odd female voice as if from a distant bomb explosion. 'What nonsense are you talking! I have not married a beggar. Hoi! Don't go after some nasty, dirty, cheap mimicry! What a degrading vow! I have to safeguard the dignity of my family!' James recognized Treesa's angry tone. His father-in-law and brothers-in-law laugh at that beggar from their mansions. And, during a visit to the Lady's Club, Treesa overhears a conversation between two 'society ladies'. One says, 'I saw that egotist Treesa's husband begging in my neighbourhood. What a shame! What a pity!'

Treesa weeps. Treesa is hanging her head in shame. Treesa's cheeks are burning with self-contempt. Her mind is fuming. Really, really, a scandalous downfall. But James does not care about what they feel. He doesn't care a hoot about it.

James enters a house with a begging bowl. It was the thirty-first house. There, a fashionable young lady is shocked to see James. She comments to somebody in a low voice: 'Now where's that ostentatious Treesa's boasting pomp?'

James enters the next house. A young man there can't believe that scene. He exclaims, 'Look at him! Is he not the brother-in-law of that business tycoon Francis?'

Without paying regard to these remarks, James completes his fortieth house visit. Then James asks himself, 'What next?'

The hallucinatory future scenario came to a close. A shudder passed over him. At that time, he perceived two different dark coloured rays piercing his eyes. One is deep red. It's his better-half, Treesa. Treesa is the advocate of resplendent mundane materialism. The other is deep green. It signifies his Mom and Nature and tells him about the soul, and spiritual obligations. Both the colours with their characteristic deep hues suffocate him.

The green colour warns: 'Oh, James, do remember fully well that the face you are fondling now is not yours; the limbs, of which you are proud are not yours. The laughter you laugh out is not yours. Those all belong to those generous saints who answered promptly your devoted mother's earnest prayers. Just, just remember that!' Right then, with a jerk, his soul jumps out of his body and sees that its orphaned body has fallen onto a bed of sharp nails. Shocked he asks himself, 'Who is breaking the bonds of agreement? Who is wounding one's own crucible?

Yes, James is his name! Now James slips uncontrollably on the smooth surface of love and self-respect, like an unguided ballistic missile. Exactly at that moment, the voice of his intense interior attitude vibrates at the tip of his tongue loudly, 'Please, please, forget me forever!'

Then with deep affliction and mental agony, he realizes that his debilitated body is lying on the trajectory of flashes of lightning and crashes of thunder. Lying there, the body looks to that direction through which the sword of judgement would descend with a deep blaring sound.

However, James manages to overcome that awkward predicament of hallucination. He gets up with a throbbing burst of energy. James goes to the storeroom, takes out a big bowl and a pair of shredded clothes He covers his head with a piece of black cloth. He stands in front of the large mirror in a gloomy mood. James asks himself, 'James, where are you going today?'

James answers without any hesitation, 'I am going to beg alms from door to door of forty houses in order to perform the vow of Mom. Its sole aim is my health and longevity.'

With that, two scenes appeared before him. In the first scene, Treesa is flying away from him, leaving him. In the second scene, Treesa has expelled him forever from her mansion. James walks away. 'Okay, that does not matter at all,' says James to himself. 'What matters most is my full lifespan, my full life span, my full life span alone.'

$$\frac{55\,\text{o}}{\frac{19}{300\,\text{p}}}$$